6/6,

# DANNY GLOVER

# DANNY GLOVER

❧

*Gloria Blakely*

*CHELSEA HOUSE PUBLISHERS*
*Philadelphia*

**Chelsea House Publishers**

*Editor in Chief*        Sally Cheney
*Director of Production*  Kim Shinners
*Production Manager*     Pamela Loos
*Art Director*          Sara Davis
*Production Editor*      Diann Grasse

**Staff for DANNY GLOVER**

*Senior Editor*          John Ziff
*Associate Art Director*  Takeshi Takahashi
*Layout*                21st Century Publishing and Communications

The Chelsea House World Wide Web address is
http://www.chelseahouse.com

First Printing

1 3 5 7 9 8 6 4 2

CIP applied for ISBN 0-7910-6285-6

# CONTENTS

❧

# BLACK AMERICANS OF ACHIEVEMENT

HENRY AARON
*baseball great*

KAREEM ABDUL-JABBAR
*basketball great*

MUHAMMAD ALI
*heavyweight champion*

RICHARD ALLEN
*religious leader and social activist*

MAYA ANGELOU
*author*

LOUIS ARMSTRONG
*musician*

ARTHUR ASHE
*tennis great*

JOSEPHINE BAKER
*entertainer*

TYRA BANKS
*model*

BENJAMIN BANNEKER
*scientist and mathematician*

COUNT BASIE
*bandleader and composer*

ANGELA BASSETT
*actress*

ROMARE BEARDEN
*artist*

HALLE BERRY
*actress*

MARY MCLEOD BETHUNE
*educator*

GEORGE WASHINGTON
CARVER
*botanist*

JOHNNIE COCHRAN
*lawyer*

BILL COSBY
*entertainer*

MILES DAVIS
*musician*

FREDERICK DOUGLASS
*abolitionist editor*

CHARLES DREW
*physician*

PAUL LAURENCE DUNBAR
*poet*

DUKE ELLINGTON
*bandleader and composer*

RALPH ELLISON
*author*

JULIUS ERVING
*basketball great*

LOUIS FARRAKHAN
*political activist*

ELLA FITZGERALD
*singer*

ARETHA FRANKLIN
*entertainer*

MORGAN FREEMAN
*actor*

MARCUS GARVEY
*black nationalist leader*

JOSH GIBSON
*baseball great*

WHOOPI GOLDBERG
*entertainer*

DANNY GLOVER
*actor*

CUBA GOODING JR.
*actor*

ALEX HALEY
*author*

PRINCE HALL
*social reformer*

JIMI HENDRIX
*musician*

MATTHEW HENSON
*explorer*

GREGORY HINES
*performer*

BILLIE HOLIDAY
*singer*

LENA HORNE
*entertainer*

WHITNEY HOUSTON
*singer and actress*

LANGSTON HUGHES
*poet*

JANET JACKSON
*musician*

JESSE JACKSON
*civil-rights leader and politician*

MICHAEL JACKSON
*entertainer*

SAMUEL L. JACKSON
*actor*

T. D. JAKES
*religious leader*

JACK JOHNSON
*heavyweight champion*

MAE JEMISON
*astronaut*

MAGIC JOHNSON
*basketball great*

SCOTT JOPLIN
*composer*

BARBARA JORDAN
*politician*

MICHAEL JORDAN
*basketball great*

CORETTA SCOTT KING
*civil-rights leader*

MARTIN LUTHER KING, JR.
*civil-rights leader*

LEWIS LATIMER
*scientist*

SPIKE LEE
*filmmaker*

CARL LEWIS
*champion athlete*

RONALD McNAIR
*astronaut*

MALCOLM X
*militant black leader*

BOB MARLEY
*musician*

THURGOOD MARSHALL
*Supreme Court justice*

TERRY McMILLAN
*author*

TONI MORRISON
*author*

ELIJAH MUHAMMAD
*religious leader*

EDDIE MURPHY
*entertainer*

JESSE OWENS
*champion athlete*

SATCHEL PAIGE
*baseball great*

CHARLIE PARKER
*musician*

ROSA PARKS
*civil-rights leader*

COLIN POWELL
*military leader*

QUEEN LATIFAH
*entertainer*

DELLA REESE
*entertainer*

PAUL ROBESON
*singer and actor*

JACKIE ROBINSON
*baseball great*

CHRIS ROCK
*comedian and actor*

DIANA ROSS
*entertainer*

AL SHARPTON
*minister and activist*

WILL SMITH
*actor*

WESLEY SNIPES
*actor*

CLARENCE THOMAS
*Supreme Court justice*

SOJOURNER TRUTH
*antislavery activist*

HARRIET TUBMAN
*antislavery activist*

NAT TURNER
*slave revolt leader*

TINA TURNER
*entertainer*

ALICE WALKER
*author*

MADAM C. J. WALKER
*entrepreneur*

BOOKER T. WASHINGTON
*educator*

DENZEL WASHINGTON
*actor*

J. C. WATTS
*politician*

VANESSA WILLIAMS
*singer and actress*

VENUS WILLIAMS
*tennis star*

OPRAH WINFREY
*entertainer*

TIGER WOODS
*golf star*

# ON
# ACHIEVEMENT

———— ❧ ————

*Coretta Scott King*

Before you begin this book, I hope you will ask yourself what the word *excellence* means to you. I think it's a question we should all ask, and keep asking as we grow older and change. Because the truest answer to it should never change. When you think of excellence, perhaps you think of success at work; or of becoming wealthy; or meeting the right person, getting married, and having a good family life.

Those goals are worth striving for, but there is a better way to look at excellence. As Martin Luther King Jr. said in one of his last sermons, "I want you to be first in love. I want you to be first in moral excellence. I want you to be first in generosity. If you want to be important, wonderful. If you want to be great, wonderful. But recognize that he who is greatest among you shall be your servant."

My husband knew that the true meaning of achievement is service. When I met him, in 1952, he was already ordained as a Baptist minister and was working toward a doctoral degree at Boston University. I was studying at the New England Conservatory and dreamed of accomplishments in music. We married a year later, and after I graduated the following year we moved to Montgomery, Alabama. We didn't know it then, but our notions of achievement were about to undergo a dramatic change.

You may have read or heard about what happened next. What began with the boycott of a local bus line grew into a national crusade, and by the time he was assassinated in 1968 my husband had fashioned a black movement powerful enough to shatter forever the practice of racial segregation. What you may not have read about is where he learned to resist injustice without compromising his religious beliefs.

He adopted a strategy of nonviolence from a man of a different race, who lived in a different country and even practiced a different religion. The man was Mahatma Gandhi, the great leader of India, who devoted his life to serving humanity in the spirit of love and nonviolence. It was in these principles that Martin discovered his method for social reform. More than anything else, those two principles were the key to his achievements.

These books are about African Americans who served society through the excellence of their achievements. They form part of the rich history of black men and women in America—a history of stunning accomplishments in every field of human endeavor, from literature and art to science, industry, education, diplomacy, athletics, jurisprudence, even polar exploration.

Not all of the people in this history had the same ideals, but I think you will find that all of them had something in common. Like Martin Luther King Jr., they all decided to become "drum majors" and serve humanity. In that principle—whether it was expressed in books, inventions, or song— they found a goal and a guide outside themselves that showed them a way to serve others instead of living only for themselves.

Reading the stories of these courageous men and women not only helps us discover the principles that we will use to guide our own lives; it also teaches us about our black heritage and about America itself. It is crucial for us to know the heroes and heroines of our history and to realize that the price we paid in our struggle for equality in America was dear. But we must also understand that we have gotten as far as we have partly because America's democratic system and ideals made it possible.

We are still struggling with racism and prejudice. But the great men and women in this series are a tribute to the spirit of the country in which they have flourished. And that makes their stories special and worth knowing.

# 1

# THE AWAKENING

"WHEN I VISITED that campus, my eyes opened up," Danny Glover recalled in 1987. "I'd never seen that type of black student before. I didn't know about Muslims before. But here was Elijah Muhammad talking about being black and self-sufficient. I wanted to learn more." It was 1966 when Danny first set foot on the campus of San Francisco State University (SFSU) in California, and young black Americans were determined to have the full benefit of each and every right expressed in the new, most comprehensive Civil Rights Act (1964) ever to be passed by the U.S. Congress. Elijah Muhammad had become the first national leader of the Black Muslims, a group that had become a major force in the civil rights movement.

The grounds of SFSU, like so many campuses across the United States, were a staging area for young people of all races to rally for their causes. And their causes were as diverse as the students behind them. In large numbers, baby boomers—those born in the period between the end of World War II and 1964, which had a very high birth rate—were acting on their political ideals to right a world they believed had gone wrong. They were the largest population of young people this country had ever seen and they were using their numbers to make a difference. On a national level, they took to the streets shouting for the protections guaranteed to minorities by law, and they were growing more vocal in their opposition to the Vietnam War. Within the confines of their campuses, black students were demanding greater racial diversity on the faculty and in the student body. Some, like Danny Glover, wanted courses on African-American culture and heritage added to the curriculum. Most of all, they wanted a voice in the way their schools were being run, and they did not hesitate to place their bodies in harm's way in order to achieve that goal. While the majority of student actions were peaceful, violent confrontations with police did sometimes occur.

Danny Glover found a world that fit him like a well-tailored suit when he walked into the politically charged environment at San Francisco State. During a panel discussion conducted by *The Nation* in 1999, Danny recalled, "You had cops out on campus every day, and you had the community and the faculty, who virtually shut the whole campus down." Though he would eventually enroll, Danny did not originally go to SFSU for an education. Instead, he intended to volunteer for a children's community program sponsored by black university students. But exposure to politics in action ignited a fire in him that would forever change his life. "Even as a student in the late sixties at San Francisco State, I saw that kind of organizing—mobilizing people around issues," says Danny.

In truth, a political conscience did not come immediately to this teenager. It took time to achieve. He had dropped out of City College months earlier. After a mere two semesters, Danny Glover knew that higher education would prove just as challenging as academics always had throughout his young life. Following his brief period at City College, Danny put a strong work ethic into play washing dishes for $1.50 an hour at a women's college called Lone Mountain. Without any game plan for his future, he moved on to a dishwashing job at Mount Zion Hospital, which paid all of $.76 more per hour plus overtime. This was the limit of his career until a friend mentioned going to State University to volunteer for a community tutorial program.

This tall, shy, awkward kid, who had been teased by fellow classmates from grammar school right through high school, was about to learn to be black and proud. When he crossed the threshold of the Black Student Union at San Francisco State University, Danny quickly saw that he could be anything he wanted to be and that he could make a difference in the world. He learned that he didn't have to be light-skinned and thin-lipped with a narrow nose to become a part of student activities. At long last, he found peers who were as concerned as he was about community improvement. Black truly was beautiful.

It didn't take long for Danny to become totally hooked on the student struggle for social change. As a consequence, he enrolled in night courses while continuing to earn a living scrubbing dishes during the day. Although reading always proved difficult for him because he suffered from dyslexia, which went undiagnosed throughout his childhood, he had an aptitude for math. So he thought a major in economics was a possibility for him. With that in mind, he became a full-time student at San Francisco State University in 1967, but continued to apply much of his spare time to tutoring inner-city students. Who more than Danny Glover, for whom reading was so difficult, knew the importance of reading? He once told a conference of teachers, "Education . . . interests me greatly and I'm sure that a lot of it has to do with my being dyslexic and having an undiagnosed learning [disability] as a child."

Danny also volunteered his time to the Western

Addition Community Organization, which helped people displaced by urban development. During the 1960s and 1970s, sections of numerous black neighborhoods were torn down to make room for highway projects, upscale development, and large public housing tracts. At the same time, many private service providers seemed to fade from low-income areas, making it necessary for communities to establish programs to help fill the gap.

Just over the bridge from San Francisco, in Oakland, Huey P. Newton and Bobby Seale created the Black Panther Party, which provided free breakfasts and lunches to neighborhood children and made sickle-cell anemia testing readily available to local residents, among other projects. However, in the public's eyes, the Panthers' provocative rhetoric and gun-toting image frequently outweighed their community service mission. Nonetheless, the party's humanitarian work did not go unnoticed by Danny. Although never a member, he did help with the Panthers' San Francisco breakfast program at a Catholic church and supported other initiatives.

Danny was becoming a man who could approach new adventures with curiosity and enthusiasm. "What I saw . . . was amazing," he said. He was just beginning to understand the breadth of influence one human being could have. For example, revolutionary poetry read by Sonia Sanchez and Huey Newton quickly captured the attention of young minds, Danny's included. So when political activist and writer Amiri Baraka wanted revolutionary thinkers to join his plays, Danny was ready to answer the call. "They needed actors for a play called *Pappa's Daughter* and I volunteered, having never been onstage in my life," he says. "I was completely tongue-tied in the audition." Despite Danny's modest description of his first steps into the world of entertainment, his audition was good enough to win him a part.

Baraka, formerly known as LeRoi Jones, came to
San Francisco State University to mount experimen-
tal plays demonstrating an outspoken perspective on
the worth of black people. Danny's introduction to
acting began with the earthy and candid words of
Baraka's short dramas. "I did activist roles in many of
the plays," Danny explained. "I felt I was making a
statement in the plays." The powerful words of
Baraka, Frantz Fanon, James Baldwin, and Nelson
Mandews, along with other young social leaders,
helped fan the flames of political activism that
burned inside of Danny. "My [acting] interest began
simultaneously with my political involvement,"
he said. "My acting is also an extension of my

involvement in community politics, working with groups like the African Liberation Support Committee, tutorial programs, etc. All of these things, at some point, drew me into acting."

During the late sixties, political expression frequently turned violent on the streets of the nation's cities. Years of racial tension boiled over into riots that required large numbers of police officers or state National Guard units to quell. For many blacks, especially among the young, the promise of a more just society at some point in the future was no longer enough. They wanted to live in a better world right now.

The same feeling of urgency echoed across universities. Though by comparison most political demonstrations on college campuses were less disorderly and only rarely led to bloodshed, violence did sometimes break out. Danny Glover made the fight for racial equality his passion. Having mastered dramatic dialogue on stage, Danny was no longer too shy to voice his opinions in front of fellow students. He spoke at rallies in the Black Student Union where he was a member. He participated in organizing a strike to block the decision to eliminate the university's ethnic studies department. The strike resulted in his arrest, along with about 400 other students, but did not deter him from struggling to better the community around him. For a time, he coordinated three reading centers for children. His acting led to chairmanship of the Black Student Union's new art and cultural committee. In 1970, his political vigor made him the obvious choice to chair the entire BSU. However, the greatest revolution during his matriculation at San Francisco State probably was within his soul, for he learned to recognize that he could make a difference.

By 1971, Danny left college to accept a position as an evaluator of community programs for the mayor's office in the city of San Francisco. Looking

back on those days, he reminisces, "My friends had graduated, and the intensity on the campus was gone. The student strike was behind us. A new student population was coming in. The job allowed me to help in the community. My great vision was to eventually develop economic projects in a third-world country, maybe Zimbabwe or Tanzania." Danny had come to embrace Pan-Africanism, a concept that encouraged people of color worldwide to support one another in the global struggle for political freedom and economic self-determination. This philosophy would help shape his future.

*A University of California student is pushed to the ground after attempting to cross a picket line formed by Black Student Union members and other students, February 4, 1969. The civil rights movement and opposition to the Vietnam War galvanized college campuses in the late 1960s and early 1970s.*

# 2

# ROOTS OF ACTIVISM

❦

DANNY GLOVER IS the oldest son of James and Carrie Glover. Born on July 22, 1947, Danny spent his early years in rural Georgia. This was the heart of "Jim Crow" country, where blacks and whites were kept separate by law and by long tradition. If there was any doubt about the racial rules, signs on restaurants, movie theaters, bus stations, and rest rooms made the situation perfectly clear: "For whites only" or "Colored" adorned almost all public facilities. In the late 19th century, after the Civil War had done away with the institution of slavery, the United States Supreme Court had ruled permissible legal separation of the races, as long as the facilities provided each race were equal.

However, particularly in the rural South, it was easy to see that separate was anything but equal. Life for African Americans meant cherishing whatever you were able to get, such as small, dilapidated schools with minimal books and equipment. It meant walking carefully among whites because the slightest perceived provocation might lead to a lynching. For that reason, black children were trained to be silent around adults. They were further taught to be unobtrusive and humble regardless of the insults forced upon them. They had to bite their tongues and accept the laws and social conditions that restricted them.

Still, during the modern civil rights movement, a groundswell of opposition to racist laws arose. The

*Cotton sharecroppers work a field in Georgia, 1937. Shortly after their son's birth, Danny's parents left their farm in rural Georgia and headed to San Francisco in search of a better life.*

National Association for the Advancement of Colored People (NAACP) was only one of the groups that began challenging racism early in the 20th century. When a crack NAACP legal team was formed to battle biased regulations in state and federal courts, the issue of racial equality in the United States was thrust onto the world stage. Sit-ins, marches, and boycotts would spread nationwide in support of the legal challenges. Just a few months before Danny Glover came into this world, the Congress of Racial Equality (CORE) and the Fellowship of Reconciliation formed a biracial group of 23 students to openly disregard segregation rules on interstate buses. They had decided it was time for blacks to sit anywhere they chose and not be restricted to sitting in the back of the bus. The first "freedom ride," on which black passengers openly defied laws requiring them to sit in the back or stand if a white person needed a seat, got under way in April 1947.

The Glovers left Georgia in the early days of this civil upheaval. No doubt, James and Carrie Glover moved their family to San Francisco, California, in search of a better life for themselves and their son. They arrived impoverished and had to make a home in a government housing project in the Haight-Ashbury district. While not as obvious or as all-encompassing as what they had known in the South, the Glovers encountered a certain degree of racial separation in their new home in California. Blacks resided on different streets. They attended predominantly black schools or, within integrated schools, were grouped together in classes. When it came to career advancement, opportunities were very hard to come by.

However, in California this racial segregation was the result of social convention, not Jim Crow laws. In California, as in other northern and western states, African Americans had the same legal rights as nonblacks. This reality gave black Americans outside the South more hope for the future, as well as more room to operate in the present. The Glovers could compete for

a broader range of occupations in California than they could ever expect in rural Georgia. Their children would be freer to simply be themselves and to become whatever they wanted. Despite the fact that such a move would bring drastic changes to their lives, opportunities for happiness in California were too irresistible for the Glovers to forgo.

In San Francisco, the family embarked on the road to a better life. Both James and Carrie obtained jobs with the U.S. Post Office. They divided their time between working, raising their five children (two boys and two girls joined Danny in the Glover family), and lending a helping hand in their community. They were also active members of the NAACP. Danny was able to observe his parents' style of taking care of business with heavy doses of love and good humor. After years of hard work and careful money management, the Glovers'

*Signs like this one littered the landscape of the South before the Supreme Court dismantled Jim Crow. Summer visits to his grandparents' Georgia farm brought Danny face-to-face with virulent prejudice.*

*A street in San Francisco in the 1960s. Life in the California city brought better opportunities for the Glover family, but Danny's teen years weren't blissful: he suffered constant teasing from schoolmates and struggled with a learning disability.*

financial situation began to improve. When Danny was 10 years old, the family moved out of the projects and into better housing.

For Danny, however, this move didn't necessarily signal the beginning of a happy time. He was a skinny kid whose body grew faster than the rest of the children his age. His awkwardly tall appearance, coupled with Negroid features made him a prime target for relentless teasing by other youngsters. As a consequence, Danny spent most of his youthful days in San Francisco as a shy outsider. "[K]ids would pick fights with me all the time. I was teased because of my height," Danny remembered. He continued, "I felt uncomfortable at dances and certainly didn't have any girlfriends. My only serious girlfriend in high school was someone named Frances, and she'd been everybody else's girlfriend before she was mine."

His poor academic performance in school only added to Danny's sense of inadequacy. Though he worked hard, he barely kept up with the rest of the class. Reading was his biggest problem. His ability to comprehend schoolwork was greatly hampered by his dyslexia, a condition in the brain that can jumble letters or words, making them unrecognizable. For dyslexics, letters or entire words can be reversed. A "b" may be seen as a "d," or "saw" may appear to be "was."

When Danny was growing up, dyslexia often remained undiagnosed. In his case, the condition wasn't identified until his early thirties, well after his school years. Because of his dyslexia, Danny did far better in academic areas that involved the least amount of reading, such as math. "I was a failing student in almost every subject except math," he says. "Math came easy, and it was my saving grace since third grade."

Dyslexia may have slowed him down, but it didn't stop him from what he truly wanted to do. He once stated at a teachers' conference, "Maybe my episode with dyslexia is not as critical, is not as debilitating as others, but you make accommodations." Later, he added, "You make certain adjustments and you recognize that the information you're seeking is much more important than the obstacles that prevent you from getting it."

Danny not only remained in school, he found a way to make money. At age 11, he took a job delivering newspapers before his classes. "Jobs offered tangible results," he explains. "If you asked my customers, they'd tell you I was the best paperboy in the city. I got up at four-fifteen every morning so that their paper was delivered before they left for work. We're talking good tips and at least $150 a month."

Football was another outlet for the teenage Danny. As a football player, his size provided an edge. Playing the position of tight end, he coupled his height advantage with the strong work ethic instilled in him by his parents. Unfortunately, his football glory was cut short by the onset of epileptic seizures at age 16. (Danny would continue to suffer from epilepsy, a disorder usually caused by an abnormality in the brain, until his seizures mysteriously stopped at age 30.) With football permanently off the table, Danny developed other interests.

Although he enjoyed singing in the church choir, acting before an audience was not on the radar screen at this time.

Like most teenagers rushing to be in control of their lives, Danny Glover wanted to learn about the world outside the safety of his home and away from the direction of his loving parents. His curiosity took some unusual turns. He occasionally drove the family car to North Beach to watch flamenco dancers, who fascinated him. Flamenco dancers carry themselves proudly erect, as messages tapped by their feet to a rapid Spanish beat pass between male and female partners. During the course of the performance, male dancers, in formfitting costumes with ruffled shirts, turn elegantly around their partners, who respond likewise while swinging flowing skirts.

At other times Danny's interests were less artistic. Sometimes, for example, he would hang out in pool halls. "I once lost my newspaper profit rolling dice in a pool hall and have never gambled since," Danny said, admitting that he expressed teenage angst in some very self-destructive ways. "I did a lot of dumb things as a kid—joyriding, shoplifting. I was arrested several times as a juvenile. The last time my father picked me up at the police station. I saw him cry." The Glover family is a close-knit group. Danny describes his father as "his best friend and one of the kindest people I've ever met." He adds, "My dad harbors no anger toward anyone. He's not threatened by your space." Danny inherited much of his father's quiet grace, but it was not always evident during his teenage years.

Fortunately, with his father as a strong role model, Danny took a step back and got a picture of where he was headed. There was nothing impressive about his illegal activity and where it was taking him, so he wisely ended his delinquent ways.

Despite the frustration, despite the dyslexia, and despite the epilepsy, Danny somehow managed to graduate from high school in 1965. Still, he was pretty

*Danny's high school yearbook photo. When he graduated in 1965, Danny had little direction in his life.*

much clueless about his future. His mother was the first in the family to graduate from college. Accordingly, college seemed a sensible choice for him, if he could find one that would accept his poor high school grades. He realized that he hadn't left himself a lot of options for higher education. "When you didn't know what to do, you went to City College," he said. Danny's experience with that institution lasted all of two semesters. He dropped out of school without the slightest idea of what he wanted from life. Any dreams he may have harbored remained unspoken and too unclear to influence his daily actions.

# 3

# WILL THE REAL DANNY GLOVER PLEASE STAND UP?

**❦**

SOMEWHERE DEEP INSIDE of him, the real Danny Glover was aching to walk in the light of day. He had a burning desire to show more than flashes of his true self without worrying if people would still accept him. In the confusion of searching for his identity, a teenage Danny tried positive as well as negative paths, and at times he seemed simply to be treading water.

Danny had been raised in two worlds. During most of the year, he lived with his parents in urban San Francisco. Over some summers, however, he went to stay with his grandparents on their farm in rural Louisville, Georgia. The experience gave Danny not just a strong blue-collar foundation but also a wider perspective on the struggles of ordinary people. Life in both environments fostered a sense of work as its own reward, along with powerful humanitarian ideals. Despite occasional detours, the strong models of his parents and grandparents endowed Danny with a drive to serve a meaningful purpose in life. "Often as a kid you try to pick people who remind you of yourself," he told the *Philadelphia Tribune* in 1994 about his selection of role models. Danny merely needed validation of his family's down-to-earth approach from the larger world outside his family.

His second-grade teacher, Ms. Lumber, saw

*Danny and his wife of more than 25 years, Asake Bomani, attend the 2000 Emmy Awards. The two met as students at San Francisco State University.*

beyond Danny's superficial aspects of dyslexia and skin color. She "honored our own particular uniqueness and individuality," Danny would explain to a conference of teachers. When she selected him to be the class milk monitor, he accepted it as "a civic responsibility, and in the second grade, it doesn't get better than that." That kind of leadership comes with "responsibility and power, a sense of ownership." However, affirmation of Danny's abilities by peers and other adults occurred too sparingly to sustain the confidence given to him by Ms. Lumber.

Years later, washing dishes for a meager wage was hardly living up to the leadership potential he cherished as a seven-year-old child, especially not when so many young people had struggled for so long to bring about social change in America. Danny grew up with TV images of civil rights marches and other acts of nonviolent confrontation. Every stroke of the soapy brush against the grain of dirty dishes carried with it those scenes of African-American men, women, and children linked arm in arm, singing songs of freedom before they were confronted with dogs, batons, and fists.

Memories of racial discrimination didn't just disappear. The long drives from California across the South were made unforgettable because beyond the borders of Arkansas the Glovers were afraid to stop their car until they had pulled into the family farm. In five trips made between 1954 and 1969, the all-night drive from Arkansas to Georgia remained a necessity. Once in Georgia, the family had to go to the back door to use restrooms and had to eat at separate lunch counters. Such experiences stayed as much a part of Danny in San Francisco as they did on his grandparents' farm. "The pain of it exists," says Danny. "You wear it, you walk with it, you hold your head up high, and certainly greater people than myself—including my grandparents and my mother and father—have held their heads up high in spite of it."

For Danny Glover, being embraced by student activists at San Francisco State University permanently lifted his head up against the gnawing pain of racism and prejudice. This 19-year-old dropout first walked on the campus of San Francisco State to tutor children in a university-sponsored youth program, but he left campus a well-rounded young man. As his involvement in community improvement projects increased, his academic goals, likewise, came into clearer focus. He decided to work toward a degree in economics. Laboring as a custodian and washing dishes helped pay for his education. Taking leadership roles in the campus fight for an African-American Studies department and for student rights helped nurture his spirit.

Before becoming a student leader, Danny discovered another way to voice radical political opinions. As he explained in 1994, socially progressive messages could be delivered through acting:

> My acting is also an extension of my involvement in community politics, working with groups like the African Liberation Support Committee, tutorial programs, etc. All of these things, at some point, drew me into acting. Amiri Baraka came out here in 1967 and was looking for somebody to do some acting in some plays he was putting together. At the time, it was a new outlook for Black theater.

His activist roles in the political and social statements of Amiri Baraka were not going to win him any Tony Awards. Those roles did not call for stellar acting technique as much as they drew on raw emotional expression. He learned the true meaning of acting when he joined a community theater group headed by actor Mel Stewart. "Mel showed us there was more to acting than going on stage and making faces," Danny explained. "He worked with us on improvisation and offered lessons in akido [a form of Japanese martial arts] to improve our concentration. Still, it was just a community activity. I was planning to pursue acting about as much as I was planning to send my resume to IBM. Hey, I was into changing society. I was into the revolution."

His days at San Francisco State were eye opening, but his worldly experience was still pretty much limited to one city in northern California and a country farm in Georgia. He was just getting to know the world around him when a peace-, love-, and drug-fest started cooking in his old stomping grounds of Haight-Ashbury. In the spirit of the times, he followed his beliefs wherever they happened to take him. For a few revelatory months in 1968, they drew him to a commune. "I came through an explosion . . . something about the music, the people," he remembered. "I really believed in living in the commune! I wasn't someone who spent most of his time trying to decipher Ibsen or whoever, but who spent his time in a very small world that was a part of a larger world." It was his commitment to the larger community that kept him firmly rooted in the student movement for civil rights.

Back on campus, Danny made another discovery. His affinity for the revolution was actually interesting to women. "You no longer had to talk to a girl and say, 'Hey baby, why don't you come walking in the moonlight with me?' " he said. "You could talk to her about community projects, poetry, student rights." This was a good thing, because Danny had very little experience being suave and debonair.

Before the "Black is Beautiful" movement, his dark skin and Negroid features seemed to turn girls off, but that situation changed dramatically after the movement began. "There was a new black

*Danny's first acting experience came in a play written by Amiri Baraka (pictured here), who was known for creating strong black characters.*

consciousness," Danny says. "The blacks with wide noses and thick lips were in—the more African you looked, the better. The guys who had pointed noses, thin lips, light skin, wavy hair were out. A new image of the black man had come in and I fit the mold. That really improved my self-esteem." However, when it came to putting that newfound self-esteem to the test, Danny didn't jump into the mating game as quickly as he did the revolution.

Asake Bomani was a young English major at San Francisco State to whom Danny was seriously attracted. He remembers waiting outside her English class to talk with her, and he was anything but smooth. According to the Internet site *mrshowbiz.com*, he barely got out a very self-conscious, "Hi, how ya doin?" before making a hasty retreat. Only after weeks of trying to start a conversation did he finally succeed in calling and asking her out. Asake says they went for a bike ride and that she saw him every day after their first date. In the African language of Yoruba, Asake means "favorite one"; Bomani, in the African language of Swahili, means "warrior." For Danny, Asake, a native of Wilmington, Delaware, was a true reflection of her name, and it was love at first sight. "I have always been infatuated with Sake. She has a strong sense of morality, coupled with a strong sense of herself," Danny said. The two were married in 1975 and made their home in San Francisco.

When student activism on his college campus began to fade, Danny seized an opportunity to continue the inner-city work he so enjoyed by taking an administrative job for the city of San Francisco evaluating housing and education programs. A fellowship granted in 1971 also thrust him into the workings of the planning commission on zoning for the city of Berkeley. By the mid-1970s he returned to a position associated with an area of lifelong interest. He became an evaluator for youth and adult reading programs. Ironically, he still didn't understand why some words on a page appeared jumbled to him and came out wrong. Nevertheless, he was determined to see that other people got the help they needed to become accomplished readers.

Within a year after their marriage, Asake and Danny became the proud owners of a Victorian home in Haight-Ashbury, a few blocks from the neighborhood of his youth. Around this same time, while Asake pursued her own career as a jazz singer, Danny reacquainted himself with the world of performance art. While evaluating a social program, he saw a notice about a community theater looking for actors with improvisational experience. "I answered it out of curiosity," he admits, "but I really liked it and the wheels began to turn." It wasn't long before he was regularly receiving roles at the Black Box Theater Company, and he attended the Black Actors' Workshop in the renowned American Conservatory Theater. "I kind of felt my way into it," he explained to *Newsweek* in 1998. "There are so many talented cats around, so much of it was luck."

Soon Danny Glover was hooked on acting. His pride and joy, daughter Mandisa, was born in 1976 immediately after Danny caught the acting bug. Although the name Mandisa is South African for "sweet," her father spent so many nights rehearsing and performing at the theater that she became known as "the workshop baby." Danny's life was quite full with a family, a daytime civil service job, and nighttime activities at the theater.

Soon Danny began thinking about shifting his entire career to the job he wanted most—acting. "I was gaining confidence," he says, "but could I really do this for a career?" After all, he had a family to support. Danny discussed the alternatives with Asake. "Thank God for Yellow Cab," Danny said. "When I found out I could drive a cab and make $100 a day, I was in seventh heaven. I could do whatever I wanted to do."

Around 1977, the 29-year-old family man said good-bye to his secure government job and began driving a cab from 4:00 A.M. to 2:00 P.M. This left him free to pursue casting calls as far away as Los Angeles, in addition to winning roles at the local theater. "My goal," he said, "was to take in a hundred dollars in taxi fares each day and still have time to prepare myself for an audition. That meant I had to drive that cab like it was the last cab on the planet. I was consistently bringing home two

*A scene from* Escape from Alcatraz, *starring Clint Eastwood. Though he had only a bit role, Danny made his film debut in the 1979 prison drama.*

thousand dollars a month, more money than I'd ever made as a civil servant." Driving the cab was a breeze for Danny, but dyslexia made preparation for auditions and subsequent roles more challenging. Researching the characters and the eras in which they lived, as well as memorizing lines, required considerably more time and concentration from Danny than the average actor needed. Nevertheless, he persevered until he got his big break.

His stage career had given him the opportunity to prove that he could handle a variety of roles. Danny's appearances spanned classic plays like

*Macbeth*, to newer works, such as *Nevis Mountain Dew* or *Suicide in B Flat*. Eventually Danny saw living in San Francisco, away from the business opportunities afforded him in Hollywood, as problematic. So he and Asake took a leap of faith: they packed up their belongings and, with Mandisa, headed downstate to Los Angeles, where Danny could be closer to the action. With his family's livelihood riding on it, Danny threw himself into his work full-time. In 1979, *Escape from Alcatraz* marked his film debut. He only had a small role, but it was a start toward bigger things.

# 4

# WHAT COMMITMENT
# CAN BRING!

❧

In the 1985 film The Color Purple, *Danny took on a complex—and controversial—character. His portrayal of the violent, mean-spirited, and small-minded Mister ignited a firestorm of protest from the African-American community.*

FOR THE GLOVERS, life in Los Angeles was anything but secure. It alternated between success and failure. Danny added a number of television appearances to his credits, including guest spots on *B.J. and the Bear, Paris, Lou Grant,* and *The Greatest American Hero.* He found film roles in *Chu Chu and the Philly Flash* in 1981 and *Out* in 1982. Such successes were interspersed with periods of making ends meet by scooping ice cream behind a soda fountain. "For several years, I ranged from being seriously broke, not being able to meet my bills, to making more money in a few months than I ever had in my life," Danny said of those times. "But I knew I was close. Something big was going to happen."

Of all the acting parts during the lean years, Danny seemed most drawn to plays that dealt with racial unrest in South Africa. Dramatic roles in *Island* and *Siswe Banzi is Dead* fanned the political flames that always smoldered inside him. This social awareness, coupled with the fact that he grew up with American-style discrimination, made the plays of Athol Fugard doubly appealing. They gave him the opportunity to again combine art with political expression as he had in college many years earlier.

Fugard's plays embraced a timely subject that was rarely discussed at American dinner tables—race relations in South Africa. In South Africa the white minority maintained its power and privileged status through apartheid, a policy of racial segregation and political and economic discrimination against all non-Europeans. The apartheid laws, passed in 1948, virtually guaranteed that most blacks would spend a lifetime in poverty while white South Africans enjoyed the wealth that came from the nation's highly productive mines, factories, and farms. Unwilling to accept this oppression, many South Africans took up the struggle against apartheid, fighting with guns as well as words. Exiled black artists such as Mariam Makeba and Hugh Masekela exposed the injustices of the system, as did white writers such as novelist Alan Paton and playwright Athol Fugard.

In his plays, Fugard usually managed to develop a black character who walked with grace and dignity through the racism swirling around him. Such fictional characters were not unlike Nelson Mandela, a real lawyer, freedom fighter, and leader of the African National Congress (ANC), who spent more than 25 years in a dismal South African prison for his efforts to dismantle apartheid. It was those types of compelling characters that enthralled Danny Glover.

Danny was so dedicated to Fugard's work that in 1980, while playing the lead in an off-Broadway production of *Blood Knot*, he turned down what could have been his big break. He was offered a role in the television pilot of *Hill Street Blues*. Unfortunately, he had no understudy in *Blood Knot*. Knowing that his acceptance of the *Hill Street Blues* part would force the Fugard play to close, he maintained his first commitment. "I found in this beautiful piece of political poetry a more human way of saying the same things I had performed as part of the more strident, agit-prop theater in college," Danny said. "Here was a real play with characters and not just positions." His character's "humanity and justice became what I wanted," Danny added.

Although he was later given a recurring role in the highly successful *Hill Street Blues*, he knew a critical

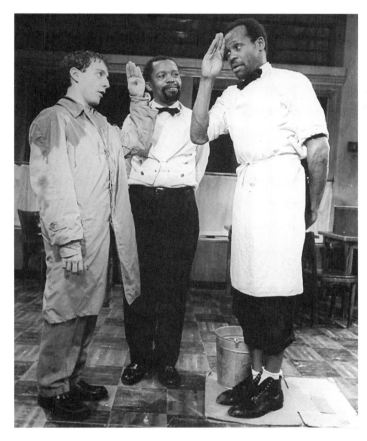

*Danny, with Lenny Price (left) and Zakes Mokae, in a scene from Athol Fugard's* Master Harold . . . and the Boys. *His performance as Willie garnered Danny critical acclaim and a Theatre World Award.*

door had closed and that such an opportunity might never come again. That decision also left him and his family living with minimal income in New York City, where Danny's call to the stage had taken them. Still, there is a saying that every good deed is its own reward. During the run of *Blood Knot*, playwright Athol Fugard saw Danny Glover's performance and was so impressed that he offered the actor the starring role of Willie in the premiere of *Master Harold . . . and the Boys*.

Before a big premiere on Broadway in New York City, directors often work out the bugs in a play at smaller locations. In this case, performances were held at Yale University Repertory Theater in New Haven, Connecticut. When the big night on Broadway arrived, the performance went off without a hitch. In critiquing the play, Frank Rich of the *New York Times* wrote, "[A]s easygoing Willie, Mr. Glover is a paragon of sweet kindliness—until events leave him whipped and sobbing in a chair, his low moans serving as forlorn counterpoint to the play's main confrontation." Happily, his parents were able to share in the success of Danny's Broadway debut in a leading role. He even paid for his father to fly in for the New York premiere. Critical approval of his performance followed rather quickly as Danny won a 1981–82 Theatre World Award.

Little did he know when he captured the Broadway stage in this 1981 three-person play that his big break was about to arrive. After witnessing Danny's acting abilities onstage, director Robert Benton selected him for a major role in the dramatic film *Places in the Heart*. This 1984 motion picture became the event that elevated Danny's career to a new level.

In the movie Academy Award–winning actress Sally Field plays the recently widowed Mrs. Spaulding, who is barely holding onto her family and land during the height of the Great Depression in 1935. Then Moses, played by Danny Glover, comes along. He suggests putting the land to work for her. Side by side, this white woman and black man plant 30 acres of cotton, thereby saving Mrs. Spaulding's farm. There is no way to properly thank Moses for his efforts, so in the end she simply says, "Moze, you took a no-count piece of land and a bunch of people who didn't know what they were doing and you farmed that land better than anybody could, colored or white. You're the one who brought in the first bale of cotton this year. Don't you ever forget that."

From the beginning the role, which was rewritten especially for him, reminded Danny of summers on his grandparents' farm, "picking cotton and trusting in . . . God," as he once described life with his grandfather. Danny's Georgia experiences helped him to

breathe realism into every fiber of the character of Moses. When handling the mule and fighting to bring in the cotton crop, Danny wanted his grandfather to see him doing it right. His grandparents got a look at the final product after Danny bought them a tape and VCR.

His mother did not survive to see Danny's movie career take flight, however. In 1983, only days before filming began for *Places in the Heart*, she died in a tragic automobile accident. But her spirit remained with him throughout the production. At the end, Moses bestows gifts on the Spaulding household as a way of saying good-bye to a life that might have been. He gives Mrs. Spaulding a handkerchief that belonged to his mother, a scene that brought Danny's real mother to mind. "She was with me in so many ways," he said. "I mean, she was there when I gave the handkerchief to Sally. . . . I think as actors, we

*Acting opposite an established Hollywood star put Danny's movie career on the fast track. In 1984's critically acclaimed* Places in the Heart, *a movie set during the Great Depression, he shared the screen with Oscar winner Sally Field.*

probably would have found ways to get what we wanted, but what happened with my mother gave us the thrust. At a time I was mourning, it gave me strength." On the strength of its cast and director, *Places in the Heart* became a box-office success.

The movie dared to explore several controversial themes. An ensemble of actors, which also included Ed Harris and John Malkovich, led audiences into the great racial and gender divides, carried them through the dark corridors of marital relationships, and toyed with the broad possibilities of what makes a family. In the film's first few minutes, Sheriff Spaulding is accidentally killed by a drunken black boy playing with a gun. Then the poor child is tied to the back of a pickup truck and dies after being hung from a tree by some "upstanding" townsfolk. While the Spaulding house is still filled with mourners, Moses comes to the door.

After the widow Spaulding takes over financial and physical responsibility for her land, she has to stand toe-to-toe with sexist male bankers and cotton brokers in order to get a fair deal. Gender issues are mixed with story lines on marital infidelity between neighbors. The film also chronicles the makeshift family that arises in the Spaulding house consisting of Moses, an unrelated blind man (John Malkovich), Mrs. Spaulding (Sally Field), and her two children. For the efforts of everyone involved, the movie received 11 Academy Award nominations, including Best Picture, one of the highest forms of recognition in the film industry.

Danny was obviously proud of this drama. Yet as serious as its messages were, he retained a sense of humor about his work. While joking about the film's success, he said, "I haven't stirred an ice-cream soda since." There was certainly no need for a job as a soda jerk, because in the same year he made *Places in the Heart*, Danny added *Birdy, Iceman, Witness,* and *The Stand-In* to his movie credits.

In *Witness*, the most popular of the four movies, Danny stretched his thespian skin into the role of a corrupt narcotics cop from Philadelphia who has committed a murder and wants to eliminate the only witness, an Amish boy who is being protected by the film's lead character, played by Harrison Ford. Danny showed the movie's director, Peter Weir, and filmgoers everywhere that he could infuse a villain with subtle ferocity just as effectively as he built empathy for a hero. Like *Places in the Heart*, *Witness* caught the attention of the Academy of Motion Picture Arts and Sciences, which doled out several Oscar nominations to the film.

The following year, in *The Color Purple*, Danny took on the highly controversial male lead, Mister, alongside Whoopi Goldberg as Celie. The movie, based on the Pulitzer Prize–winning novel of the same name by Alice Walker, takes an unflinching look at African-American life. Some of its characters, particularly Mister, are distinctively unappealing.

Mister is a complex character. From birth he has felt the weight of his father and the weight of the white world bearing down on him. He vents all his pent-up anger and frustration on his wife, Celie, and her sister, Nettie—who he feels are merely around to serve him. Danny's portrayal of the violent, mean-spirited, and small-minded Mister was met with protests from many people in the black community, including the NAACP, which detested the film's negative perspective on black men.

Danny took the criticism in stride because, in developing this fictional character, he looked deep into the heart and mind of Mister, and found a unique individual, not a stock character intended to represent all black men. Danny saw the role as "the most challenging written for a black actor in a long time." It was a role, he told the *New York Times*, "I wanted real bad, anyone would." He saw Mister as a product of physical and emotional abuse, who then mimicked

*With Whoopi Goldberg in a scene from* The Color Purple. *Though the character was distinctly unappealing, Danny brought depth and subtlety to his portrayal of the abusive Mister.*

this abusive behavior in his relationship with his wife. Nevertheless, another side of his personality comes into sharp focus when his longtime love, Shug, enters the household. Danny says about Mister, "We're all products of our social environment. That dictates how we act, the attitudes we have." He added, "When Shug was in his presence, he was like a little boy. If he could maintain that feeling he had when Shug was there, he would be O.K." To Mister's dismay, he can't have the one thing he idealizes. In response, he intensifies his mistreatment of Celie for not being Shug and for the loss of his wistful idealism. In a way, all of the furor that surrounded the role of Mister could be viewed as a backhanded compliment to Danny's ability to introduce enough life into a character to stimulate strong and lasting emotions in its viewers.

It's hard to understand where Danny Glover got

the references for playing one of the novel's most disturbing characters. Unlike Mister, both Danny's parents and grandparents had long, loving marriages. "I have a 91-year-old grandfather and his relationship with my 90-year-old grandmother has been glorious for 70 years. They worked, they built, they grew!" he said. "I have that to draw on." When describing his parents to the *New York Times*, he said they were "hand in glove—they loved each other, you could see it in their eyes. . . . They were so interdependent. When my mother died, my father didn't know what to do. When Celie left, Mister didn't know what to do." Danny was able to look at his family experience and turn it upside down to create the insecure character he portrayed in the film. Despite the contentious relationship between Mister and his wife, Mister relies upon Celie to help define himself. Without realizing it, his attachment to her has become quite strong. "Celie's departure from Mister was like death for him, like they cut off his arm," says Danny in explaining the depth of his portrayal.

Danny followed his appearance in *The Color Purple* with a heroic role in a Western, *Silverado*. In that film, director Lawrence Kasdan cast Danny as Malachi, an eagle-eyed, rifle-toting drifter returning home to his father and sister. Along the way, he meets other gun-slinging wanderers heading in the same direction. When Malachi finds his father's homestead burned down by neighbors who want to possess all the farmland around the town, he and his straight-shooting friends reluctantly join forces to rid the area of these ruthless and despicable people.

After the release of *Silverado*, children would come up to Danny with fingers pointed like guns and quote his memorable line, "I don't want to kill you and you don't want to be dead." This epic Western launched Kevin Costner's career and kept Kevin Kline's popularity on track.

By the time *The Color Purple* and *Silverado* hit

the big screen in 1985, Danny knew he had made it in Hollywood. He was already lined up to do a selection of movie, theater, and television projects. "I like the new freedom to choose my next role, but I don't really want to feel secure," said a thoughtful Danny at the time. "I don't mind feeling that everything is tenuous. It keeps me up and in shape."

Workaholic or not, Danny strives to maintain some level of normalcy in his life. With his name firmly embedded in the minds of casting agents and directors, he moved his family back to their Haight-Ashbury home, where the neighbors saw him simply as Danny, the husband, father, son, and brother. His exit from Los Angeles was not a choice most rising actors would make, but show business was only one part of his life. If he had to decide between an Academy Award nomination and his family, being a father and husband would come first. In a 1986 interview, he discussed how his wife and daughter gave him a sense of purpose. He derived strength, he said, from getting up in the morning with certain responsibilities, being with his wife for 14 years, and "just watching Mandisa grow up. I get a certain sense of self out of that, and I enjoy it."

The downside of the move away from Hollywood was the long six-month absences from home to film a movie. They were the toughest part of show business for this family man. To ensure that his daughter received enough fatherly attention during her youth, Mandisa often visited him on location. On those occasions, he would take her to museums and tour other notable sites. "That's how I balance out the time we are together and the time we are not," he said. "She's been on location with me for *Witness* and for about six weeks during *The Color Purple*. . . . I have to make adjustments in my life whenever I'm not on the road to take into consideration her particular needs." Mandisa seems to thrive on the attention from her father. *The Color Purple* became

her favorite Danny Glover film. At 10 years of age she said, "I think he was mean, but he played it well."

Meanwhile, Asake continued to pursue her own entertainment career as a jazz vocalist. The similarities in their work help explain the respect they share for each other's line of business. Danny says, "We like giving each other their space. . . . She certainly has her life and I wouldn't want her to feel that she has to be a stepchild to what happens with my career." Basically they were both happy in their careers and accepted the related demands on their time. However, after 10 years of paying his dues in show business, Danny's career was finally coming together. Now, they would all have to adjust to more frequent departures, because Danny's train had left the station and was picking up speed.

*Silverado played well to fans if not critics. Pictured here from the 1985 Western are, from left, Kevin Costner, Scott Glenn, Kevin Kline, and Danny Glover.*

# 5

## BRINGING IN BIG BUCKS

&

AS THE SCRIPTS rolled in, Danny knew he was fast becoming a role model for millions of Americans. With a newfound ability to choose his parts, he sought to strike a balance between projects that reflected his social and political beliefs, projects with responsible messages, and projects with the potential to become huge box-office hits. His response to heated debates surrounding the film version of *The Color Purple* demonstrates his commitment to maintaining this balance. "It's important for the NAACP and other organizations to question the film," Danny said. "It makes us actors more conscious of what we're doing. And that's all positive."

Danny believes that we all have an enormous power to heal and shape the world around us. His mission as an actor and human being is to promote that feeling of empowerment and strength in others. "My whole idea of theater when I became involved in it was using theater as a way of informing people," Danny says. "I think that you have to reach people in so many creative ways, ways that go beyond. If you can reach them through music, if you reach them through poetry, whatever way in which you are able to reach them I think is important. What I should do more than anything else [as an actor] is reinforce our belief in humanity."

*Burgeoning popularity didn't stop Danny from taking on roles that had social value but little blockbuster potential. Here he portrays South African human rights activist Nelson Mandela in the HBO Pictures presentation* Mandela.

So how do movies like *Lethal Weapon* fit into this ideal? Through four films starting in 1987, Danny has played Roger Murtaugh, a Los Angeles homicide detective and family man who is perpetually on the verge of retiring. Packed with explosions, car chases, and characters that dispense rounds of ammunition like candy, the Lethal Weapon movies would never be confused with, say, an Athol Fugard play.

Yet the movies have been extremely lucrative. Each has raked in profits approaching $100 million. In addition to the action-filled scripts, much of the credit must go to the chemistry between the two costars, Danny Glover and Mel Gibson. In contrast to Gibson's hyper and perpetually on-the-edge character, Martin Riggs, Danny's character, Roger Murtaugh, is level-headed and somewhat restrained. As film critic Roger Ebert said in 1988 about Danny's performance in the original *Lethal Weapon*, "His job is to supply the movie's center of gravity, while all the nuts and weirdos and victims whirl around him." He did that quite well, and, as Ebert observed, *Lethal Weapon* made Danny a huge Hollywood star.

Still, some might wonder how the role of Roger Murtaugh squared with Danny's liberal politics. During *The Nation's* recent panel discussion, Danny was asked how depicting a heroic officer in the Los Angeles Police Department fits with actual reports of widespread racism and the public's perception of the department as a "racist police force, little better than an army" occupying a foreign country. He responded, "It's a very, very, very difficult thing—it's almost like I become apolitical when I do this. On the one hand you want to applaud the potential of what you believe could be good law enforcement, and certainly the relationship between these two cops, one white and one black, stands out. The analysis of the department itself doesn't become

the focus, as opposed to the things it's fighting against. We tend to look at these officers as individuals, aside from their work as part of this force of occupation. It's almost as if they are above this in some way."

If the politics of the movies don't quite mesh with Danny's views, there is still a positive

*Danny and Mel Gibson in a scene from the original* Lethal Weapon. *The success of the series has transformed Danny into a huge star and given him the financial security to produce his own films.*

underlying message in the social realm, and it finds expression in the relationship between the two main characters. Following the release of the first *Lethal Weapon*, Danny explained, "After seeing *The Year of Living Dangerously* [a film that starred Gibson] twice, I wanted to work with Mel. He has an honesty that you can't teach. I read the script and I loved the relationship between the two guys. And I loved the fact that the white character comes to the black person's home. Usually, we see it the other way around. The only problem was that the violence was too gratuitous at the end." Violence aside, while the cameras were rolling, a chemistry developed between the characters that was a blend of brotherly and fatherly affection.

Danny was performing on stage in Chicago in 1986, when he got the call to read with Mel Gibson for *Lethal Weapon*. He used his day off from the play, Athol Fugard's *A Lesson from Aloes*, and traveled to the Los Angeles home of producer Richard Donner. Unlike Danny's first audition at San Francisco State almost 20 years before, he could say with complete confidence that the reading with Gibson went well. The two immediately clicked.

Off the set, the two actors liked each other but had little in common. Danny was well settled with a family, while Gibson was young and still living the single life. Like the characters they played, the two formed a more enduring bond with the passage of years, the filming of several sequels, and Gibson's marriage. Now they get together between movies for lunch and stay in touch with each other's lives. Gibson told *Jet* magazine, "I've never been able to explain our relationship except for the fact that I 'get him' and he 'gets me.' He's considerate, generous and a brilliant actor." He added, "Our advantage in this case is that we really do enjoy each other's company; we do understand and like these characters, and we do have a tremendous relationship with the filmmakers. We can put that up on the screen with complete integrity."

The comfortable relationship between detectives Murtaugh and Riggs may have first attracted Danny to the *Lethal Weapon* set. But he has reprised his role largely because the formulaic series has enabled him to make big bucks. And that financial security in turn has given him the freedom to carefully select other roles and to produce films with high social value.

One such film is the made-for-cable movie *Mandela*. Danny played the title role of Nelson Mandela, the lawyer, freedom fighter, and African National Congress leader who was imprisoned for 27 years by the white supremacist South African government. Alfre Woodard costarred as Winnie, Mandela's wife. In the few years they lived together, Mandela was repeatedly arrested for promoting nonviolent protests against the state. Finally, he made one of the hardest decisions of his life—to defend his people by force of arms—when the government continually responded to peaceful ANC actions with murderous violence.

After the movie's release, Mandela was finally released from prison and, in South Africa's first fully democratic and nonracial balloting, won the nation's presidency. For his portrayal of this incredible leader, Danny Glover earned the NAACP Image Award, and both he and Woodard won Cable ACE Awards.

Even before taking the role, Danny knew the story of South Africa all too well. From a continent away he had done what he could to support the South Africans' march to freedom. *Mandela* gave him an opportunity to send their messages to a wider audience than his stage performances previously allowed. The strength of Danny's acting ability is profoundly illustrated in the scene when Mandela explains his departure from non-violence:

> Friends, this is the choice—either we submit or we fight. Your leaders have been driven underground, but they will still lead. We will never desert you. I am here to tell you that although Congress is now banned, we will never stop meeting, organizing, planning. The fight, the real fight is only just begun. In this country, there are two worlds—for whites a democracy, for non-whites a colonial power crawling on crutches out of the middle ages. Well, we will make one world and we will bring them into a new age whether they like it or not. . . . Self-defense is a right. I shall fight the government side by side with you, inch by inch and mile by mile until victory is won. . . . You come along with us or remain silent and neutral in this matter of life and death. For my own part, I have made my choice. I will not leave South Africa, nor will I surrender.

Mandela and other ANC leaders were convicted of treason and sentenced to life imprisonment.

Winnie Mandela had been trained as a social worker rather than a revolutionary, but she could not remain silent or let her husband's sacrifice be forgotten. She mobilized a youth force to fight apartheid and was jailed for about a year and a half. That experience only strengthened her resolve to end white supremacy. Such efforts were coupled with a growing international outcry to end apartheid.

As far back as 1982, the O'Jays, a group of African-American male singers, asked fellow performers to boycott South Africa "as long as the evil apartheid system is in place in that country." The group's spokesperson told *Jet* magazine, "We

have been there to witness the humiliating and dehumanizing effects of the system, and we have wanted to express these feelings ever since returning, but didn't because the time was not right. However, the time is right now."

That same year, Robert S. McNamara, the former U.S. secretary of defense and president of the World Bank, predicted that white minority

*Nelson Mandela with his wife, Winnie, upon his release from Victor Prison in Cape Town, South Africa, Sunday, February 11, 1990.*

rule would be overthrown in South Africa within 20 years. He urged the United States to clearly state that it would not aid the white government when the racial explosion occurred.

In 1984, after Pope John Paul II met with South African prime minister Pieter W. Botha, the Vatican publicly condemned racial segregation in that nation. It said that the Roman Catholic Church considered apartheid contrary to Christian principles. Meanwhile an international cultural and economic boycott of South Africa began to gather momentum.

Black South Africans and supporters around the world shouted for the release of Nelson Mandela, which they felt would demonstrate the government's good-faith intention to resolve the issue of apartheid. Finally, in the face of constant unrest at home and mounting pressure from abroad, the South African government offered Mandela his freedom. But in exchange, he had to agree to refrain from all political actions against the government.

Mandela refused to consent to the deal. At the conclusion of the cable movie *Mandela*, Danny Glover powerfully articulates the ANC leader's stunning message to his people: "I cherish my own freedom dearly, but I care even more about your freedom. Too many have died since I went to prison. Too many have suffered for the love of freedom. I'm no less life-loving than you are, but I can not sell my birthright, nor am I prepared to sell the birthright of the people to be free. . . . Your freedom and mine can not be separated."

South Africa had long been a part of Danny's life both on and off the stage. After Mandela's election to the presidency, Danny explained his past commitment to a group of Africans: "Your struggle has been my struggle. I supported your efforts from afar by raising money for your liberation efforts, by informing people about your struggle and encouraging them to get involved."

However, not all Americans felt the same way. When Vice President Cheney was secretary of defense, news reports indicated that he took a stance against freeing Nelson Mandela. Prior to the airing of the HBO film *Mandela* in 1987, American right-wing conservatives, including the Reverend Jerry Falwell and an organization called Citizens for Reagan, threatened boycotts against the movie and its film company. They reportedly viewed the movie as Communist propaganda and as proterrorist. In the end, however, HBO chairman Michael Fuchs stood his ground and let the viewing audience decide this film's merits. Other film projects about the South African struggle, such as *Cry Freedom*, followed suit.

By the time the 1980s came to a close, Danny Glover had spread his wings in a number of provocative directions. Most rising stars focused their attention on the big screen, but not Danny. He had found a freedom of expression in television that was hard to re-create in big-budget feature films. In television, he had the opportunity to play Walter Lee Younger in a film centered on American race relations in *A Raisin in the Sun*. He happily took on the role of Alex in *Dead Man Out*, an HBO movie about capital punishment. His interest in the lives of children never waned, as evidenced by his hosting and narrating of *Storybook Classics* for child TV viewers. He approaches television work with the same dedication he gives to feature films, and his abilities have been acknowledged. In 1989 he was nominated for an Emmy for Outstanding Actor in a Miniseries or Special for his depiction of Joshua Deets in the cowboy epic *Lonesome Dove*. Later that year the second installment of the money-making Lethal Weapon series was completed. The 1990s would bring two more Lethal Weapon sequels, along

*The 1989 film* Lonesome Dove *landed Danny an Emmy for Outstanding Actor in a Miniseries or Special. Despite his success in feature films, Danny has maintained a regular presence on television.*

with much more work of which Danny could be proud.

While Danny was establishing full control of his career, Asake would parlay her experience managing an art gallery into her own business. She transformed her love of African art, which found expression in her private collection at home, into a popular art gallery on trendy Post Street in San Francisco. Bomani Gallery opened in December 1991 with 2,000 square feet in which to feature the works of black artists from around the globe.

# 6

# IN THE DRIVER'S SEAT

❦

DURING THE 1990s, Danny Glover fully realized his goal of using show business to inform people in many creative ways. Danny had his hands on a wide range of ventures to spread his special brand of humanity through almost every form of communication. His audiences were not limited by age. Both young and old have enjoyed and benefited from his efforts. Children are used to hearing his voice or seeing him host educational programs. His desire to engage them in learning has not faltered since his college days, when he tutored individual youngsters in reading. His forum of communication has simply gotten bigger. For example, he went high-tech by lending his voice to a number of Aesop's fables that were placed on CD-ROM. He is often seen hosting and narrating enlightening youth series on cable TV and on PBS television stations nationwide. In 1990, Danny not only hosted and narrated the classic story *Br'er Rabbit and the Wonderful Tar Baby* for Showtime TV, he also coauthored a book to accompany the video version.

Perhaps one of his most challenging jobs was hosting and narrating the follow-up to the famed documentary *Scared Straight*. This sequel, called *Scared Straight 20 Years Later*, explored what had happened to the 17 delinquents and nine convicts

*Danny directs "Override," an episode of the Showtime series* Directed By. *As an actor, producer, and director, Danny has demonstrated his diverse talents in front of and behind the camera.*

in New Jersey's Rahway State Prison seen in the original. Danny could relate to the delinquents because, after all, he was no teen angel.

The idea behind the original *Scared Straight*, filmed in 1978, was that if they were confronted with the possible consequences of continued delinquency and crime—a prison sentence with hardened offenders—the teens might change their ways. The 17 youngsters were brought to Rahway State, where the convicts, in typically harsh tones, ridiculed, browbeat, and intimidated them.

During the taping of the sequel, Danny found himself emotionally drained by the dismal film location. "This prison was so depressing," he said, "I felt my bones aching. It's not a place that affirms life." He marveled at the ability of the prisoners, living in such a disheartening environment, to care enough to try to turn around the lives of troubled teens in the Scared Straight program. "These men take one step outside of themselves and tell kids, 'you don't want to go through here,' " he said. With a clearer respect for the entire reform program, Danny was able to add an understanding presence to the documentary.

As Danny's list of educational projects grows, he hasn't let his television work for kids deter him from undertaking children's feature films. He teamed with the Disney Company to star in several comedies. *Angels in the Outfield* (1994) and *Operation Dumbo Drop* (1995) were well received. He also made an appearance as a mountain man in the 1997 adventure film *Wild America*, starring teen heartthrobs Jonathan Taylor Thomas and Devon Sawa. Danny's experience in TV narration, along with his movie celebrity, carried him into two animated 1998 blockbusters from DreamWorks. In *The Prince of Egypt*, an impressive story based on the biblical Moses, he was the voice of the character Jethro. In *Antz*, about insects working on an ant farm, Danny supplied the voice of the hilarious soldier ant Barbatus. His familiarity with one of the owners of DreamWorks, Steven Spielberg—who directed him in *The Color Purple*—probably didn't hurt his selection for those roles.

When he wasn't captivating a new generation of minds, he was sharing pearls of wisdom in entertaining films for grown-ups. He hit the mark as a profound gas station attendant, Simon, in the quirky movie *Grand Canyon* (1991). Just as in *Silverado*, his sage character played well against the lost soul of Kevin Kline. Danny also scored big in his reprise of the Roger Murtaugh character in *Lethal Weapon 3* (1992). Then he went to the opposite end of the cop-versus-criminal spectrum by playing a bank robber in the film revival of *Maverick* (1994).

As Tyrone Kipler, a judge who is immune to bribery, Danny shared the screen with Matt Damon in *The Rainmaker* (1997). Damon starred as Rudy Baylor, an inexperienced young attorney who vows to put a stop to a ruthless insurance company victimizing poor, trusting Americans. The supporting role of the judge in this thriller garnered Danny an NAACP Image Award nomination.

Having made his mark in feature films, Danny also showed his talents in the recording industry—not by singing, but by reading. Although many of his narratives are for children, in 1997 he gained his greatest recognition from his recording of *Long Walk to Freedom: The Autobiography of Nelson Mandela*. It seemed appropriate that Danny should receive his first Grammy Award for a subject so dear to his heart. His achievement is all the more remarkable because he continues to struggle with dyslexia.

The production of each new *Lethal Weapon* film seems to grow increasingly complex. *Lethal Weapon 4*, released in 1998, required 16 cameras to capture the opening stunt, which involved Murtaugh and Riggs taking out a psychopath holding a machine gun in one hand and a flamethrower in the other. The two cops take care of business with the help of an exploding gasoline truck. For another stunt, the newly built Highway 215 in Nevada was closed for two weeks. The ever-more-complicated action sequences seem to have paid dividends at the box office: each new *Lethal Weapon* movie has surpassed the previous one in ticket sales. During its first weekend in 1998, *Lethal Weapon 4* pushed to the top of the box-office list, grossing $34.4 million.

Still, no actor can go through an entire career without a few failures. One of Danny's less-glowing roles was that of a serial killer in writer-director Jeb Stuart's 1997 film *Switchback*. Likewise, his well-played role of Gus alongside Joe Pesci in the comedy *Gone Fishin'* (1997) did not light up box offices as expected. Although *Gone Fishin'* was a financial disappointment in the theaters, it and Danny's other Disney movies signaled a different type of success. More than 15 years earlier, Disney had struck a deal with the NAACP, promising to increase representation of blacks in its movies. African-American actors are still walking through the door opened years ago by leading civil rights activists.

Although a string of financial failures can doom an actor's career, Danny has successfully balanced crowd pleasers like *Predator 2* (1990), *Flight of the Intruder* (1990), and *A Rage in Harlem* (1991) with artistic endeavors. In *Bopha!* (1993) he shows the inner turmoil of a South African police officer sworn to defend the government in the face of his love for a son fighting against apartheid. *The Saints of Fort Washington* (1993) saw Danny and Matt Dillon depicting the lives of the urban homeless.

Danny continues to be in demand for feature

films of all types. It isn't surprising to see him in a Western one year and in a modern-day thriller the next. He brings his formidable talents and hard work to each part, and generally makes it look easy. Alfre Woodard, who starred with him in *Grand Canyon, Bopha!*, and *Mandela*, said, "Acting with Danny is like a comfortable slow drag, where you wrap your bodies together and feel each other's heat."

Indeed, the mellow Danny heated up the screen

*An intense moment from* A Rage in Harlem, *1 of 12 feature films Danny appeared in during the first half of the 1990s.*

in some memorable—if not richly successful—films of his own making. In 1990, he completed a project that some critics called his best work. *To Sleep With Anger* is a satiric drama akin to the biblical tale of the serpent tempting Eve with the forbidden fruit. In this case, Harry Mention slithers into the home of trusting Christians and proceeds to turn their world upside down. Danny starred as the smooth-talking sinner from the Deep South. Beneath Harry's down-home charm stands a man whose greatest thrill is using people's insecurities against them. Although *To Sleep With Anger* never had the potential to be a huge box-office success, it is typical of the risks Danny is willing to take not only as an actor, but also as an executive producer.

If any man has the ability to carry the load of both producing and starring in a film, Danny proved he has it in *To Sleep with Anger*. Local residents of South Central Los Angeles were disgruntled by the disruption that came with shooting the film in their neighborhood. Blocked-off streets and lines of trucks with equipment, food, costumes, and the stars' quarters were too much for some locals. Rather than getting upset by the complaints, Danny took time to circulate through the community and chat with its residents. His warm, entertaining nature proved enough to ease the tension. Then, at the close of production, he revealed another side of his talents. Apparently Danny has skills in the kitchen. He used them to whip up enough seafood gumbo to leave the crew, cast, and people in the neighborhood feeling quite satisfied.

Since that time, he has built Carrie Production, a company he started in 1986, to enable him to deliver powerful films about the rarely told lives of heroic blacks. These are stories like the one conveyed in *Deadly Voyage* (1996), in which Africans stow away on a Russian freighter heading from Ghana to France. In fear of losing their jobs for not

*With Paul Butler in the 1990 film* To Sleep With Anger. *Besides starring in the film, Danny served as coexecutive producer.*

detecting the stowaways before the ship left port, the crew members kill eight of the nine Ghanaians. The film is a thought-provoking look at how much people will risk for a chance at a better life—or to maintain the life they already have.

Starting in the late 1990s, there have been more movies focusing on blacks than in any time in the history of the motion picture industry. Hundreds of new multiscreen cinemas have been added to the thousands already in operation across the country. Demand to fill the screens of local cineplexes has given broader opportunities to independent films. Gone are the days when major movie studios controlled the handful of black directors with limited potential for financial backing for a production. Old favorites John Singleton and Spike Lee are now joined by George Tillman Jr., Debbie Allen, Charles Dutton, Wesley Snipes, Danny Glover, and others. Most of them are managing relatively low-budget films with socially relevant themes. Some projects involve TV movies carrying options for theater release before their television premiere. To the public's benefit, many of these productions are works of art that go well beyond lightweight exploitation films. Films about black professionals and black families have raked in millions of dollars from ticket sales. *The Best Man* ranked among the top five money-makers during its initial release. *Soul Food* brought in $45 million from moviegoers. However, today's movies pass through theaters so quickly that the bulk of the revenue for black films comes from television releases and, more important, home video sales.

Danny Glover can take credit for *America's Dream* (1996), *Deadly Voyage* (1996), *Buffalo Soldiers* (1997), *Freedom Song* (2000), and *Boesman and Lena* (2000), to name just a few of his HBO and TNT productions. These and other independent works have given audiences choices for viewing quality films of a type not previously available. If there is a universal theme running through these movies, it is blacks battling against racism in their quest for dignity, self-respect, and the fulfillment of a personal dream.

With the assistance of his family, Danny's dream of creating meaningful films has become a reality. His brother Martin helped conceive *Buffalo Soldiers*, and Danny often works with his daughter, Mandisa, in the development of his projects. Not that he suffers from any shortage of acting roles,

In Buffalo Soldiers, *Danny played a member of the legendary all-black cavalry units that fought Indians and outlaws in the Old West. In conjunction with TNT, he turned the well-received film into an educational program for youngsters.*

but Danny usually finds a pivotal character for himself in Carrie Production films. He starred as Sergeant Washington Wyatt in *Buffalo Soldiers*, the historically based story of the Black 9th and 10th Calvary. Commissioned to fight in the Indian Wars and to defend American settlers in the West from marauding criminals, these all-black units were respectfully nicknamed buffalo soldiers by the Native Americans. Legend says that they never lost a battle or a man fighting the Indians. However, some met their deaths at the hands of not-so-color-blind settlers whom they fought to protect, an irony that gives Danny's film much of its unusual richness.

With such an inspiring subject, why stop at a mere film? Danny couldn't, and neither could TNT. Together with Turner Learning, a division of TNT, the *Buffalo Soldiers* movie was transformed into an educational event. Free curriculum materials were distributed to enrolled educators or accessed through the TNT website. Danny led a history lesson following a screening of the movie at Roberto Clemente Junior High School in Harlem, New York. This was vintage Danny Glover. Not just a star, he showed he was the same humanitarian who never missed an opportunity to help educate.

Danny doesn't always take a starring role in the films he produces. In *Freedom Song,* he shone in a supporting role (and earned an Emmy Award nomination). He played the father of Owen Walker, a young student determined to stand firm against the racial traditions in his rural Mississippi town.

The movie tells of Owen's unbridled enthusiasm for action and his coming to grips with the nonviolent discipline of civil rights activists from the Student Nonviolent Coordinating Committee (SNCC). Most of all, *Freedom Song* is the story of ordinary people whose moment of extraordinary conviction changed the course of civil rights in America. In one dramatic scene, Owen, played by Vicellous Reon Shannon (who also starred in *The Hurricane*), paces a jail cell packed with fellow teenage demonstrators and rails in frustration at their failure to change the rules established by nonblacks in the town. Vondie Curtis Hall, a star of the 1990s' TV series *Chicago Hope,* responds to this protest in the character of SNCC organizer

Daniel Wall. Referring to Congress CORE members heading their way, Wall says:

> Read tomorrow's paper. They saw your light. You see, I came south because I was inspired by those first sit-in students. It's like they lit a flame and I saw the light from the flame a thousand miles away. That light also inspired Freedom Riders. They carried that flame all through the South until they were stopped, but not before I saw it. It inspired you. So, you walked out of that school. You didn't just make a march. You picked up a torch and, now, other folks have seen your light, and they are coming here to carry it on because you can't right now. And, if they go to jail too, others will pick up their torch and carry it someplace else. So, you're not on your own anymore. You're part of something bigger than you. You're part of the movement.

*Freedom Song* is only one example of the extra-ordinary scripts emerging from Carrie Production.

Away from the movie set, Danny's appeal is branching into television advertising. When the Saturn Corporation wanted a believable and thoughtful voice behind its commercials launching the L series midsize car in 1999, it sought the mellow, honest Danny Glover.

Besides his voice, Danny is also in high demand because his presence adds credibility and character to any endeavor in which he partici-pates. The calls to host or participate in special events are unending. Danny does his best to respond to those that have lasting meaning. In February 2000 he gave the keynote speech at a salute to Dr. Martin Luther King Jr. In June of that year he hosted a celebration of the legendary 1938 and 1939 Carnegie Hall concerts featuring renowned black musical artists from spiritual to swing. He was the host of choice for the National Inventor's Hall of Fame induction ceremony in

*Actress Susan Sarandon presents Danny with an Essence Award, April 14, 2000. The awards are presented to individuals who have made important contributions to the lives and culture of African Americans.*

August 2000. Among others, this tribute honored Walt Disney for his patent of a special camera for filming animation, and Steve Wozniak, a founder of Apple Computer, Inc.

Danny also believes in honoring peers. He has been on stage when the entertainment industry saluted its own, such as the American Film Institute Salute to Steven Spielberg. Over the years, Danny has also appeared on stage at the Academy Awards, Tony Awards, Grammy Awards, Black Filmmakers Hall of Fame presentations, and other awards shows.

However, if the phone calls happen to slow down, there is always another project to be created by his production company. Indeed, Danny is seated squarely behind the controls of his career.

# 7

# A MAN OF ACTION

❦

"MOST PEOPLE IN Hollywood have a token thing they do, but it's mostly about self-aggrandizement and ego. That's not the case with Danny [Glover]," Mel Gibson said about his friend in a 1994 *Essence* magazine article. "He's up to his eyeballs in devoting time to community activities and just causes. He keeps going whether or not the public knows about it. He's one of the most socially aware persons around."

Looking at the range of causes for which Danny Glover struggles is almost mind-boggling. It seems more amazing considering the fact that Danny is not a hit-or-miss kind of guy. Once committed to an issue, he is in the fight until the end.

In 1993, Danny listened to a message left on his answering machine by Richard Burr, an attorney formerly with the NAACP. Burr was organizing a rally against the execution of his client, Gary Graham. After reading the details of the case, Danny got on a plane to Houston, Texas, in hopes of helping to have the execution, which was scheduled for that day, averted. Many people would have found it easy to turn their backs on a black man who admitted to choosing a career as a thief and to shooting some of his victims. But Graham denied committing the crime for which he was convicted and sentenced to die: the murder of a man named Bobby Lambert during a robbery.

*Never one to shy away from controversial causes, Danny speaks at a fund-raiser for death-row inmate Gary Graham, February 16, 1999. At right is Nation of Islam minister Robert Mohammad.*

That day in August 1993, Governor Ann Richards stayed Graham's execution. This gave Danny a chance to meet the prisoner. Danny told *Essence* magazine a year later, "Meeting him that first time was painful, [and] that kind of pain forces you to respond in some way, to do something. I made a choice to become involved in this brother's case because I could not stand the pain of not making that choice. When I went down there that first time, the only way I could relieve the pain was to do something." For almost seven years, Danny was a part of the fight to keep Graham alive. He made numerous pleas on Graham's behalf before the Texas House of Representatives, the Congressional Black Caucus, and the media. By the year 2000, some 132 executions had taken place during George W. Bush's tenure as governor of Texas. Gary Graham was added to the total despite the efforts of Danny and many others right up to the very end.

The battle for Graham's life was lost, but a larger fight against capital punishment continues. When the American Civil Liberties Union (ACLU) needed celebrity spokespersons for an Internet site calling for a moratorium on executions, Danny volunteered. Given the political climate in the United States, where a majority of people support capital punishment, achieving such a moratorium will be an uphill struggle. Yet Danny will continue lobbying, talking, and acting for this cause.

Long before joining the battle against capital punishment, Danny had supported the struggle for freedom in Namibia, South Africa, and other countries. He made his voice heard in college rallies and, later, on stage. His passion for bettering the lives of Africans has been constant in his adult life. Now his stardom grants him the means to make a tangible contribution beyond passion.

For example, the TransAfrica Forum, created by

Randall Robinson, lobbies the United States on behalf of Caribbean and African countries. For a considerable time, Danny worked with TransAfrica Forum's crusade against apartheid. After that victory was won, he and other board members of the organization raised about $1 million to support the African National Congress Party in South Africa's first democratic elections. Then, as cochair of the Fund for Democratic Elections in South Africa, Danny toured that country with other entertainers to encourage blacks to register and vote; 18 million did just that. To complete his mission for a true democracy, he returned to South Africa in April 1994 as an election observer.

Danny's passionate concern for humankind doesn't end in Africa. It extends to the welfare of people of color around the world. After the elections in South Africa, he again joined forces with the TransAfrica Forum to lobby for the downtrodden, challenging U.S. policy regarding the Caribbean nation of Haiti and Haitian refugees. Danny spoke publicly about the lack of political and economic support from President Clinton's administration for Haitians either fighting against or trying to escape oppression. In 1994, he helped gather fellow celebrities to stage a fast and demonstrate outside the White House. He also helped raise thousands of dollars for a bail bond to free five Haitian refugees jailed in Louisiana for a year until their formal request for asylum could be heard.

Danny also has a long track record as spokesperson for the Literacy Campaign and as a supporter of education. His fight for literacy for all people, which began when he was a young man in California, continues to this day. He has traveled the breadth of the United States many times, raising money and stressing the importance of reading, including parents reading to their children. He endorses the computer-aided Accelerated Reader program that is used in

*Danny poses with Lois Tinson, president of the California Teachers Association, as part of a national campaign to promote reading. Literacy has been a long-standing cause of the actor, who served as the 1999 Honorary California Chair for Read Across America.*

40,000 U.S. schools. He generously gave as much as $100,000 in his mother's name to one college.

Those civic efforts are simply the tip of the iceberg for Danny. He has answered the call for help in many other areas, including fund-raising efforts for an antidrug program in Los Angeles. Danny knows full well the importance of the war on drugs. He witnessed his brother Rodney's personal struggle against drug addiction. Danny also knows that drug dependency can take many forms. He was a spokesperson in the campaign by the cigarette manufacturer R. J. Reynolds to stop teenage use of tobacco products.

Where he finds the time and energy to immerse himself in the world's problems is difficult to tell, but his good deeds merit recognition, and occasionally such credit does come his way. Danny was among the first winners of the William Kunstler Racial Justice Award, for his personal contributions to the crusade against apartheid, his opposition to the death penalty, his support for affirmative action and minority rights, and his unending public service.

Another first came from the United Nations (UN), which knows a tireless worker when it sees one. It should come as no surprise, then, that Danny was appointed the first goodwill ambassador for the United Nations Development Programme (UNDP) in March 1998. The UN is dedicated to helping eradicate poverty in 174 countries and territories. This is to be achieved through self-help programs. In the role of goodwill ambassador, Danny worked to raise awareness of the organization's mission on all continents. One of his first orders of business was visiting UN projects in Africa that fell into four categories: economic management, poverty reduction, good governance, and small-scale enterprise development. He was pleased with the progress he saw. Women in Soweto, South Africa, were striving for economic enrichment and gender equality. The women had established a child care center, a bakery, and a basket-weaving center. In another town, new math and science curricula were being developed at a teachers training college. Throughout his tour, Danny saw African people going about the daily business of "doing for themselves." The long road to self-improvement is filled with opportunities, and with the help of UN development programs some Africans were moving forward one step at a time. Danny's goal was to set more people on that same path.

Very few people will disagree about the value of eliminating poverty and illiteracy through education and self-help programs. But as Danny has already demonstrated in protests against capital punishment, he is also willing to take on controversial issues. One such issue involves Cuba. Since the 1960s, the United States has maintained an economic embargo of the island nation, which lies off the southern coast of Florida. The tensions between Cuba and the United States date to the cold war era, when the Cuban dictator Fidel Castro was a close ally of the Soviet Union. Castro still rules Cuba, and he is still an avowed Communist, but the cold war is over and the Soviet Union no longer exists.

Still, Americans who suggest normalizing relations with Cuba typically find themselves in a political minefield. But that didn't stop Danny Glover from joining a TransAfrica Forum delegation to Cuba in 1999. The delegation denounced the continuing U.S. embargo as "unjust, unfair and cruel." Fidel Castro spent three hours discussing those matters and issues of racism in Cuba with the group.

Used to putting his money where his mouth is, Danny donated an astounding $1 million to keep the TransAfrica Forum financially sound. The organization established a $5 million campaign in 1999 to pay off the mortgages on its office building and the Arthur Ashe Jr. Foreign Policy Library. The plan is to use the remaining funds to create an endowment for future organizational programs.

The causes for which Danny Glover struggles vary so widely that finding a common thread is sometimes difficult. But whether he is speaking on behalf of the United States Tennis Association's Tennis Month or on behalf of the smaller California Network of NeighborWorks Organization, one thing bears noting: each group adds an element that is lacking in local communities and tries to bring about a better nation one person at a time and one house at a time. And Danny always seems ready to help. He simply never gives

*As the first goodwill ambassador for the United Nations Development Programme, Danny worked to raise public awareness of poverty in developing countries. He's seen here at a press conference called to announce his acceptance of the job.*

up on the capacity of human beings to improve. He says:

> I'm moved by what I see around me and encouraged by what I see in regard to people re-defining their lives and taking control of their lives. Whether that manifests in what I saw in South Africa or what I see with the young men [that were involved in gang violence] trying to maintain a truce here in L.A., or it's reflective in Boston where the neighborhood had its tenth anniversary recently as a neighborhood where the people came together as a community, a family, of some Cape Verdeans, Haitians, African-Americans, Italians, whites, Brazilians. And, they reclaimed the neighborhood. Those are the kinds of things that encourage my faith in humanity and ultimately in myself.

With that attitude, he couldn't say no when the UN Development Programme asked for his help to

*Danny hugs 11-year-old HIV patient Nkosi Johnson. Danny was in Johannesburg, South Africa, in November 2000 to support Nkosi's Haven, a center for mothers and children infected with HIV.*

increase awareness of AIDS (acquired immunodeficiency syndrome) and HIV, the virus that causes it. Danny is no doctor, but in July 2000 he stood before an international conference of health care and government professionals and talked about the worldwide spread of HIV/AIDS. The UN estimates that of the 36.1 million people around the world with HIV/AIDS, 25.3 million live in sub-Saharan Africa, while another 400,000 live in North Africa and the Middle East. AIDS has become the number one cause of death on the continent of Africa.

In African communities and other countries where its existence is often denied, Danny could put a face on the disease: the face of his brother, Rodney, who survived 10 years with the knowledge that he was infected with HIV. In places where people with AIDS are banished from their homes and stoned by family and former friends, he could tell of the support given to his brother until the day he died of rheumatoid arthritis unrelated to HIV. He could shake hands and provide words of encouragement to teenagers diagnosed with HIV or AIDS. When he witnessed the problem firsthand, it was impossible not to extend a personal donation: Danny gave $5,000 for needed expansion to a South African home for abandoned teens with HIV/AIDS, a project also supported by National Basketball Association star Dikembe Mutombo.

Of course, Danny doesn't think he can really solve all of these problems single-handedly. He simply does what he can to help. It's like throwing a pebble in a pond and watching it create a series of ripples that are many times greater than the size of the pebble and that extend in all directions. The tiny pebble that Danny or someone like him casts may get many people involved in solving a problem, and that makes the world a better place.

# 8

# KEEP ON KEEPING ON

———— ❧ ————

"THE WAY THAT blacks in Hollywood operate is to stand in line and keep your mouth shut and take the jobs that come to you," director Spike Lee told *George* magazine. "Danny doesn't do that." Added singer and actor Harry Belafonte, "I'm amazed, given his politics, that Danny has survived. Danny constantly spits in the face of betrayal, but he's been wonderfully persistent."

Persistence has been a key throughout the course of Danny Glover's career. Some of his struggles for human dignity have pitted him against major world leaders, including presidents, but he has never backed down. Danny's commitment to humankind is no passing fancy. It defines who he is as an actor and as a man. "I'd be lying if I didn't worry sometimes that my politics might hurt my career," he admits. And yet, he doesn't stop supporting the causes he feels are important, regardless of whether those causes are popular or unpopular.

He also doesn't remain silent about racism in the film industry, a business that has made it difficult for black actors to obtain work and producers to give the public a truer view of the black experience. "Danny is the guiding point for young black actors to be a formidable force," explains Themba Sibeko, a South African film producer. "He's the voice of those who don't have a voice." In a typically candid statement, Danny told *Parade* magazine, "Racial progress in Hollywood is mostly cosmetic.

Hollywood has always been a conservative place, because it doesn't consider itself art. It's about making money and getting people to buy something." Perhaps only people outside the motion picture industry—the consumers of the films Hollywood produces—can force the studios to create more opportunities for minorities.

The NAACP has threatened to organize a boycott of network television programs unless better representation of minorities is achieved. The organization will be working with the four major TV networks through the coming years to raise hiring levels of black actors, producers, and writers. Always ready to push the envelope for greater achievement, Danny exposes a shortfall in their agreement. "If we see that as progress, that's sad," he says. "Just because Blacks are in TV shows, all it means is that Blacks are buying more cars." In other words, while it's good that a few more black Americans may be visible on television, what is more important is the types of messages their presence conveys to the larger public. That is where Hollywood needs to make much more progress. When the entertainment industry refuses to take action, Danny sees an opportunity for concerned individuals to step forward and get in the game.

He and other black actors came forward with funds to help get things rolling in 1996 for Spike Lee's *Get on the Bus*. The film is the black producer-director's vivid perspective of the Million Man March for unity, which took place in Washington, D.C., in 1995. It is a unique account of the journey to solidarity by one busload of African-American men.

On the home front, the Glovers assumed ownership of a 40-acre vineyard located in Sonoma County, about an hour from their home in San Francisco. The grounds contain a cozy two-bedroom cottage accompanied by an organic chardonnay vineyard, a pool, and a stocked pond. Asake put her eye for style to work decorating the cottage with flavors from Africa to the warmth of California. "This is Asake," Glover says about its colorful interior design. "Like most husbands,

I didn't have the idea, but I'm a willing participant. I can pick things out but can't put them together."

A year later, in 1997, Danny had to say good-bye to a long-standing dream. As a young economics major in college, he developed a goal to establish a business in Africa. In 1994 Danny jumped at an opportunity to provide economic stimulus to Pepsico, a company that supported the U.S. embargo against the government of South Africa for its policy of apartheid. Danny and a block of celebrities partnered with Pepsico International and black-owned South African businesses to create a bottling company called New Age Beverages. Pepsico and the South Africans were minority owners, with 25 percent and 8 percent interests, respectively, in the firm. Danny, singing sensation Whitney Houston, NBA star Shaquille O'Neal, attorney Johnnie L. Cochran Jr., and publisher Earl G. Graves were among the star-studded American investors with a 67 percent stake in the company.

When Pepsico withdrew its business from South Africa in 1985, it held 25 percent of the soft drink market there; Coca-Cola quickly took control. After its reentry, the new company was only able to wrestle away 4.7 percent of Coke's 95 percent share of the soft drink market. Brad Shaw, a spokesperson for Pepsico, explained the situation to the *New York Times:* "It was a young, committed company competing against an entrenched monopoly. It was an important and noble experiment, but in the end the challenges were just too great. Coke's stranglehold was too tough to pry loose, and the business wasn't viable." Although the end of the experiment was a disappointment to Danny, his involvement in Africa continues.

In 1998, Danny stood squarely behind Oprah Winfrey in the making of the movie *Beloved*, an adaptation of the Pulitzer Prize–winning novel by Toni Morrison. For Winfrey, it was almost a decade in the making because no one wanted to finance an intense look at the raw emotional scars oozing from the horrors of slavery and left to fester in African-American lives

*With Oprah Winfrey in a scene from* Beloved. *The 1998 movie, based on the Toni Morrison novel, took a huge emotional toll on the actors.*

long after emancipation. Although the book did not fit Hollywood's formula for a big payday, Winfrey persisted until a backer was found. Jonathan Demme, an outstanding director with whom she had worked on *The Color Purple*, soon followed.

Demme created a chilling film that draws viewers into the very soul of the actors. As emotional as *Beloved* is to watch, the making of the movie took far more internal stamina.

Danny Glover played Paul D, the friend and love interest of Oprah Winfrey's character, Sethe. Paul D and Sethe previously shared the degradation of slavery on a Kentucky plantation ironically called "Sweet Home." When they reunite in Sethe's new residence in rural Ohio, they can't help but recount their last treacherous days of slavery. "The day we shot the scene where

Danny comes into the house for the first time and has to make that trek down the hall, something just came over him," Winfrey said. "When it was over, I could see that something had happened to him, that he hadn't come back. He was just sitting in the corner looking so out of it. I put my arms around him and said, 'Danny, what is it? You can tell me.'" Danny said he saw the destruction of the men at Sweet Home. Winfrey recalled, "He said, 'I saw Sixo being burned. I saw them all!' He said, 'Oprah, I felt them; I felt their breath.' And then he just sobbed for a long time." Danny said, "I just held on to her until I felt like I could come back."

One scene in the movie pulled a different emotion from Oprah Winfrey—fear. For months after reading the script, she lived in fear of her first on-film love scene. "The day of that scene I don't know if Danny knew how nervous I was because I was trying to act calm," she says. "But the truth is, I was a wreck. I hadn't kissed anyone but Stedman [Stedman Graham, Winfrey's longtime companion in real life] in 12 years." Demme certainly noticed the tension in her face. Between the director coaching her to relax and Danny making jokes, Winfrey made it through that scene and similar ones that followed.

*Beloved* is a multifaceted portrait of African-American relationships—something Danny Glover believes is lacking in many Hollywood films. Consistent with Winfrey's poignant style, the movie's complex relationships initiate a churning inside its characters that overflows into the exterior world. This is the type of moving film for which Danny Glover hopes to be remembered.

The start of 1999 found Danny Glover on stage once again, but not in a play about South Africa. This time he tackled a drama about a troubled interracial marriage in the 1960s between a retired African-American soldier and a frustrated Japanese wife who kicks him out of the house. This production of Philip Kan Gotana's *Yohen* brought together for the first time the East West Players, a company of artists focused on the Asian-American experience, and the Robey Theatre Company, a group of African-American artists. "This is about collaboration, about African American and Asian American theater coming together," Tim Dang, artistic director of the East West Players, told the opening-night crowd. "Because of the marriage of these two theaters, the audience will benefit the most." Dang's words captured the essence of Danny Glover's acting career—helping audiences benefit from a bird's-eye view of life.

Danny later developed a project involving his favorite playwright. He teamed with Angela Bassett to transform Athol Fugard's play *Boesman and Lena* into a movie. This was another project in which Danny flourished in the dual roles of star and producer. And because of the political changes in South Africa, this movie could be shot on location.

In *Boesman and Lena,* the political atmosphere of the times takes a backseat to interpersonal relationships. Specifically, the work examines the strain white African society places on the marriage of the title characters and how each struggles through the difficult times in vastly different ways.

On November 29, 1999, shortly after filming wrapped up, 82-year-old director John Berry died. The well-received film became a fitting tribute to his career.

The movie version is in a totally different league from the original performance of the play, by an all-white cast, in South Africa. A reviewer for *Variety* praised the film, saying, "Powerhouse performances by Angela Bassett and Danny Glover and an unusually physical approach to theatrical material are the hallmarks of *Boesman and Lena,* an excellent screen adaptation of Athol Fugard's play about a down-and-out South African couple. In the final work of his long and varied career, the late Yank director John Berry has remained faithful to the stage piece while making a real movie out of it, resulting in a distinctive film that resembles few others."

Danny didn't seem to need a break after production of *Boesman and Lena* had wrapped up. He spent

*Danny samples the fare at the November 1999 opening of Hollywood Fries in Westwood, California. The chain of eateries, in which he invested, features french fries and gourmet dipping sauces with movie-inspired names, including Godzarlic, Thaitanic, Jurassic Chili, and Lethal Weapon.*

the rest of 1999 maintaining a lightning pace that included new movie-production projects, recordings, speeches, and, as usual, commitments to worthy causes. He also bought a five-bedroom retreat in Portland, Oregon, for a reported $1.3 million. The house sits on a secluded half-acre of land in the upscale neighborhood of Dunthorpe. Of course, it's doubtful he'll spend much time actually relaxing there. Even knee surgery in September couldn't slow him down as he continued on the promotional trail using crutches.

Danny tried his luck at a totally unrelated business venture in 1999. In November, he joined a group of celebrities who invested in a chain of eateries called Hollywood Fries, which feature a menu of gourmet french fries and sauce combinations with movie-inspired names. Among the offerings: Jurassic Chili and Thaitanic.

November was also the month that an unexpected incident involving Danny caused a media frenzy. Late-night TV talk shows spewed an arsenal of jokes, but this situation was really no laughing matter. Danny, heading to downtown New York with his daughter, Mandisa, and her friend, tried to hail a cab from the corner of 116th Street and 7th Avenue in Harlem. A total of five unoccupied cabs failed to stop for the group.

A sixth cab stopped at a red light, giving Mandisa the opportunity to reach the cab door. The driver willingly unlocked both rear doors, but refused to let Danny sit in the front where Danny wanted to stretch out his six-foot-four-inch frame comfortably. After all, he had undergone knee surgery just two months earlier and reportedly suffers from a bad hip.

Danny filed a racial discrimination complaint with the Taxi and Limousine Commission in New York City. At a press conference he said, "I was so angry. The fact that my daughter's here in school, it really upsets me that if she's standing on a corner waiting to get a cab, she can't get a cab. It happens to her, it happens to countless people every day. The fact that I'm a celebrity, the fact that I'm visible, allows me to draw attention to this."

This proverbial pebble sent out ripples up and down the Hudson and Harlem Rivers. Encouraged by Danny's action, New York state senator David Paterson, who is blind, and Reverend Al Sharpton jointly filed a class-action lawsuit. Paterson said he was asked to leave more than 100 cabs after giving his home address in Harlem. Medallion cabs like the one in Danny's complaint are not allowed to refuse street fares in the city's five boroughs and certain surrounding areas.

One week after Danny filed his complaint, New York City's mayor, Rudolph Giuliani, expanded a task force called "Operation Refusal," which was started in 1996 to investigate claims of discrimination against black fares by the city's taxi fleet. On the first day of

*Accompanied by his daughter, Mandisa, Danny holds a press briefing after filing a discrimination complaint with the Taxi and Limousine Commission in New York City, November 3, 1999.*

the new crackdown, 1,761 checks by undercover officers and taxi inspectors yielded 11 violators. Six refusals were due to bias and five were based on destination. Mayor Giuliani told the press, "The cabs have been taken and summonses have been issued and the drivers have had their licenses to drive cabs suspended. I think the good news in all of this is that in the overwhelming majority of cases, the cab drivers did what they were supposed to do."

But Danny's attorney delivered an outspoken criticism of the crackdown: "I think it's the wrong application to a chronic problem, a Band-Aid on a cancer. It's a waste of resources to have black officers on corners hailing cabs." He and Danny suggested what they saw as a better solution: more training for taxi drivers beyond the required one-day cultural diversity seminar.

A spokesman for the cabbies did apologize to Danny, but the question remains: Why are some taxi drivers unwilling to pick up blacks? The most common answers are fear of being robbed and not being paid when they reach their destination. Danny Glover, who once drove a cab, told a forum of cabbies, "If a driver fears for his life if he takes a black man into his cab, then perhaps he has to have a totally different understanding of who black people are and perhaps he needs to get another job."

Mayor Giuliani has his own viewpoint. "There's a good way to avoid all of this, and that is for owners of the cabs and cab drivers just to come to the reality that life is going to be different now," he says. "I think everybody who lives in this city knows that this has been going on for a very, very long time and maybe this is an opportunity to change it."

In addition to the complaints lodged by African Americans, a significant number of complaints have been lodged against New York cab drivers by Hasidic Jews, people with disabilities, men and women with strollers, young children, and the blind with Seeing Eye dogs. Larry Carty entered the taxicab fracas with a free website (Pickusup.com) to assist these and other New Yorkers with filing complaints.

When he wasn't fighting prejudiced taxi drivers in New York City, Danny was working with Spike Lee in early 2000. Lee was the co-executive producer of 3 A.M., a murder mystery set in New York. Danny and Pam Grier costarred in this Showtime film. Oddly enough, the movie delves into the lives of three Manhattan cab drivers, one of whom is played by Danny. The cabbies are kept on their toes by the threat of a serial killer who is targeting them. Spike

Lee also drew on the writing and directing talents of Lee Davis as well as the abilities of coproducer Sam Kitt, who together made successes of *The Best Man* and *Love & Basketball*.

In August 2000, Danny became the executive producer and host of *Courage,* a television series launched for the Fox Family Channel. He wanted "to expand the whole idea of courage in the sense that as individuals, we can do courageous things," he explained. "We do things courageously every day. We want to acknowledge those things . . . and we want to show people that it's possible for individuals to change situations and circumstances." The series pays tribute to single heroic acts and the lifetime contributions of ordinary people who have done extraordinary things. This series places a different spin on reality TV programming. Danny feels the power of this series lies in the simple truth of its stories.

The month after the launch of the series, in September 2000, Danny's father, his first model of

*Spike Lee (left) and Danny share a scene in the Showtime film 3 A.M. Danny depicted a former basketball player working as a cabbie.*

*Despite reaching his midfifties, Danny Glover is as energetic and exuberant as ever. No doubt he will continue to seek out new, challenging projects well into the 21st century.*

courage, was honored at a banquet and reception. The event was part of the 44th biannual convention of the National Alliance of Postal and Federal Employees. Danny was not going to be denied a chance to give the keynote speech on an evening that paid homage to the father he loves so much. Reportedly suffering from a sprained ankle, he used a wheelchair to get into the Hilton Hotel in Los Angeles where the event was held.

Danny made his way to other business and charitable commitments despite his sprained ankle. His physical conditioning has enabled him to quickly bounce back from injuries that would have left others flat on their backs. For years, Danny has kept his body lean and muscled by managing the amount of fatty foods in his diet and riding a stationary bicycle. More recently, he began working on the "mechanics of the body." This includes the Pilates Method of fitness with one-on-one training and various specialized pieces of exercise equipment. Danny humorously promised *People* magazine, "In five years I will be in better shape than I am today. . . . Okay, if I'm not better, at least I won't be worse."

He may be unsure of bettering his physical conditioning in the future, but his unlimited courage should never be in doubt. As an actor and individual, he has demonstrated a boundless capacity to excel. Alfre Woodard told *InStyle* magazine that regardless of his accomplishments, Danny is "still the same Black hippie-dippy nationalist artsy guy."

According to Danny, he just does the things he feels are important. "I want to feel that I made choices that empowered me and substantiated me as a human being," he says. "My career is going to be here and gone. But I'm always going to be a human being. And I want to look myself in the mirror and say that I was the human being I wanted to be."

# CHRONOLOGY

1947    Danny Glover is born in Georgia to James Glover and Carrie Hunley Glover

1965    Graduates from high school in San Francisco

1966    Enters San Francisco State University; becomes community activist

1967    Performs in first play, *Pappa's Daughter*

1971    Leaves San Francisco State University; pursues civil service career

1975    Marries Asake Bomani; attends the Black Actors' Workshop/American Conservatory Theater

1976    Stage career blossoms; is drawn to the dramatic plays of Athol Fugard; daughter Mandisa is born.

1979    Makes film debut in *Escape from Alcatraz*; makes episodic TV debut in *Lou Grant*

1980    Performs lead role in *Blood Knot* by Athol Fugard on off-Broadway stage

1981    Plays lead role on the Broadway stage in *Master Harold . . . and the Boys*, by Athol Fugard; wins 1981–1982 Theatre World Award for his performance

1984    *Places in the Heart* kicks feature film career into high gear

1985    Costars in *The Color Purple*

1986    Starts Carrie Production Company

1987    Stars in *Mandela* and wins NAACP Image Award and CableACE Award for performance; costars, with Mel Gibson, in hit movie *Lethal Weapon*

1990    Stars in and is an executive producer of *To Sleep with Anger*; wins Best Actor Award from Independent Feature Project/West for performance; inducted into the Black Filmmakers Hall of Fame

1994    Cochairs the Fund for Democratic Elections in South Africa

1996    Receives a star on the Walk of Fame; is executive producer of *The Deadly Voyage*.

1998 Appointed goodwill ambassador for United Nations Development
    Programme

1999 Donates $1 million to TransAfrica Forum; stars on stage in Yohen; narrates
    TV documentary *Scared Straight! 20 Years Later*; files discrimination claim
    against a New York City taxi driver

2000 Joins UN Development Programme campaign against HIV/AIDS; launches
    TV series *Courage*; receives Essence Award for humanitarian service

# FILMOGRAPHY

| 1979 | *Escape from Alcatraz* |
|------|------------------------|
| 1981 | *Chu Chu and the Philly Flash* |
| 1982 | *Out (aka Deadly Drifter)* |
| 1983 | *The Face of Rage*<br>*Chiefs*<br>*Memorial Day* |
| 1984 | *Places in the Heart*<br>*Birdy*<br>*Iceman*<br>*Witness*<br>*The Stand-In* |
| 1985 | *The Color Purple*<br>*Silverado* |
| 1987 | *Lethal Weapon*<br>*Mandela* |
| 1988 | *Bat-21* |
| 1989 | *Lonesome Dove*<br>*Dead Man Out*<br>*Lethal Weapon 2* |
| 1990 | *Predator 2*<br>*To Sleep with Anger*<br>*Flight of the Intruder* |
| 1991 | *Pure Luck*<br>*Grand Canyon*<br>*A Rage in Harlem* |
| 1992 | *Lethal Weapon 3* |
| 1993 | *The Saint of Fort Washington*<br>*Bopha!* |
| 1994 | *Angels in the Outfield*<br>*Maverick* |

# FILMOGRAPHY

| | |
|---|---|
| 1995 | *Operation Dumbo Drop* |
| 1997 | *Gone Fishin'*<br>*Wild America*<br>*Switchback*<br>*The Rainmaker*<br>*Buffalo Soldiers* |
| 1998 | *Lethal Weapon 4*<br>*Antz*<br>*Beloved*<br>*The Prince of Egypt*<br>*Wings Against the Wind* |
| 1999 | *The Monster* |
| 2000 | *Boesman and Lena*<br>*3 A.M.* |

# BIBLIOGRAPHY

Belkin, Lisa. "Fame and Controversy for Danny Glover." *New York Times,* January 20, 1986.

Collier, Aldore. "Danny Glover: The Reluctant Movie Star." *Ebony* 41, no. 5, (March 1986).

Confehr, Clint. "Danny Glover charms teachers at Opryland Hotel Conference." *Tennessee Tribune,* February 23, 2000.

"Danny Glover, Mel Gibson, Chris Rock team up in 'Lethal Weapon 4.'" *Jet* 94, no. 9, (July 27, 1998).

Dougherty, Margot. "The Artful Lodger." *InStyle* 5, no. 7, July 1998.

Graham, Nancy Perry, and Hugh McCarten. "Insider." *People* 51, no. 14, (April 19, 1999).

Hudson, Alexis. "Conversations with Danny Glover speaking on South Africa, Hollywood & responsibilities as a role model." *Philadelphia Tribune,* September 16, 1994.

Lee, Luaine. "Like the Energizer bunny, Danny Glover just keeps on going." Knight-Ridder/Tribune News Service, November 24, 1997.

Maishah, English. "NYC sting nabs drivers for discrimination." *Washington Afro-American* 108, no. 15 (November 26, 1999).

Powell, Kevin. "What a Man!" *Essence* 25, no. 3 (July 1994).

Price, Vinette K. "Glover takes goodwill to Africa." *New York Amsterdam News* 89, no. 31, (July 30, 1998).

Schreiberg, Stu. "Down-Homes with Danny Glover." *Cosmopolitan* 203 (August 1987).

Schwarzbaum, Lisa. "Glover's Leap." *Entertainment Weekly* no. 122 (June 12, 1992).

Speace, Geri. "Danny Glover." *Newsmakers,* cumulative issue 4.

Stark, John. "Seeing red over purple." *People Weekly* 25 (March 10, 1986).

Valhouli, Christina. "Raging Against Racism." *George* 5, no. 8 (September 2000).

# INDEX

# PICTURE CREDITS

✦✦

GLORIA BLAKELY recently left a 25-year commitment to brand management in corporate America for a career in writing. She started as a journalist, contributing topical articles to a variety of national magazines and metropolitan newspapers. Her stories span topics from international travel, health, beauty, and technology to politics, the African-American legacy, and the lives of African-American artists. That experience led her to this first book for Chelsea House Publishers.

Ms. Blakely is a native of Pennsylvania. She attended the Howard University Honors Program in Psychology and was a National Merit Scholarship winner. Additional studies at Howard included African-American History. Her independent exploration of that subject continues today.

---

NATHAN IRVIN HUGGINS, one of America's leading scholars in the field of black studies, helped select the titles for the BLACK AMERICANS OF ACHIEVEMENT series, for which he also served as senior consulting editor. He was the W. E. B. DuBois Professor of History and Afro-American Studies at Harvard University and the director of the W. E. B. DuBois Institute for Afro-American Research at Harvard. He received his doctorate from Harvard in 1962 and returned there as professor in 1980 after teaching at Columbia University, the University of Massachusetts, Lake Forest College, and the California State University, Long Beach. He was the author of four books and dozens of articles, including *Black Odyssey: The Afro-American Ordeal in Slavery*, *The Harlem Renaissance*, and *Slave and Citizen: The Life of Frederick Douglass*, and was associated with the Children's Television Workshop, National Public Radio, the Boston Athenaeum, the Museum of Afro-American History, the Howard Thurman Educational Trust, and Upward Bound. Professor Huggins died in 1989, at the age of 62, in Cambridge, Massachusetts.